For Frank & Constance,
with fond memories
on new friendship in Bayreuth
Jim
Providence
September 10, 1980

Cathedral of Ice

a play by
James Schevill

Introduction by Edwin Honig

pourboire press

Editor: Peter Kaplan

1975

AUTHOR'S NOTE

This book represents the original working script of *Cathedral of Ice*. It is not intended to be read as the script for the finished version of the play that is being produced by the Trinity Square Repertory Company of Providence, Rhode Island.

ACKNOWLEDGEMENTS

The publisher wishes to thank
Luella Thompson, Pat Schwadron, Betsy Potter
and Herbert E. Kaplan for their assistance
in the production of the book.

Cover by Rebecca Edwards

L. C.   75-33465
ISBN   0-915176-10-6

The Pourboire Press
P. O. Box 315
Woods Hole, Mass.
02543

Copyright © 1975 by James Schevill
Composition and printing by the Woods Hole Press

To

*Adrian Hall, Richard Cumming, Eugene Lee, Franne Lee,
and the
members of the Trinity Square Repertory Company.*

Cathedral of Ice: A Dream Play
An Introduction by Edwin Honig

There are two main questions we will have to have answered about Schevill's latest dramatic piece. First, why is it called a "dream play"? Then, how to take Hitler, the chief actor—historical character or personal projection, imaginatively documented, of the Fuehrer's unguarded wishes, desires, frustrations? The answer to the first may turn up in puzzling out the answer to the second question.

Hitler, the actor in *Cathedral of Ice*, obviously grows out of the real man's life and deeds in the 30's and 40's, as many have known them through hard experience and the subsequent books. More important, he is a part of history we have helped him to make. With Marilyn Monroe, Richard Nixon, and other types of sex and power images afloat in contemporary reveries, he feeds on the uncontrollable facts of having been born to certain parents and being victimized by certain antagonists all his life. Neither hateful nor sympathetic, he is the human integer we cannot discard without ceasing to be living individuals.

To put it another way: Hitler becomes what he is because we admire men whose dreams turn into real schemes. But the price often paid for admiring them is the tremendous power they are allowed to brandish over us. Their place in history is largely an effect of how intensely we support their schemes, since only by becoming public do private dreams continue to burn, continue to be made.

All this is why *Cathedral of Ice* is called a dream play. While showing how "crazy" Hitler's own dreams are, the play reveals how we are drawn into crazy dreams of power. But approve or disapprove of what he does, we must also invent antagonists to drain off his charismatic power gained by embodying our dreams. We see that dreams are measured in action by the anti-dream, the factual reality they have been created to oppose. Hitler's real antagonist, is, of course, Neumann. Neumann is the brooding, disturbing presence condemned to Hitler's dream because he gave Hitler the "Jewish coat" in Viennese days. He lives on after death, a motivating antagonist in Hitler's blind assault against the Jews. Neumann is also the counterplay to this destructive force as he is transformed into the Hasidic Masters.

The line of this dream play then is that as Hitler continues to develop his vision of the *Cathedral of Ice* in 1975, the counterforces of the dream explode around him, not only in the Neumann and Hasidic figures but also in others like Roehm who demand their place in history from him. And as the dream machine (the central visual image incorporating these effects) continues to produce unguarded fantasies, we see that necessary though they are to protect his schemes, the fantasies are never quite what Hitler wants. His real self always breaks through; his essential sentimentality and banality (as opposed to the heroism we endow him with) always destroy him.

Are we destroyed too? That is a third question, implied by the play, which each of us must answer for himself.

ACT I

Scene I

(*As the audience enters the theatre they see the Dream Machine creating eerie comic and serious dream images. These dream images are taken from key scenes in the play such as the car sequence, the Old Shatterhand sequence, the songs, etc. Or the actors can improvise on images from their own dreams that fit into contemporary themes of power. The Dream Machine has a certain futuristic look, but it is also strangely archaic in appearance with obsolete, mythological panels and compartments pertinent to themes in the play.*)

NARRATOR: (*Played by the actor who will play* HITLER)

    Ladies and Gentlemen, welcome to the Dreams of Power.
    Enjoy yourselves. Dream! This is your hour.
    Do you fancy Love, Fame, Wealth?

        (*He motions to the three sections in which the audience are seated.*)

    In dream the choice is ours—let's choose our health.

        (*Here, if the actor so desires and the opportunity seems right, the actor can improvise on his most recent night or day-dream. When finished with these few lines he points to the Dream Machine.*)

    Today, for our pleasure, we live by Dream Machines.

        (*He moves closer to inspect it.*)

    I love a good machine that slaves, washes, cleans;

        (*Patting the Dream Machine*)

    A scientific gadget that produces any dream I wish:

        (*Two actors as a car appear from the Dream Machine*)

    My dream car fast and sleek . . . (*He drives his car.*)
    My favorite dish. . .

        (*He's served with an all-American ice cream cone out of the machine.*)

    Talk shows and pro football on TV
    And movies like they used to make for me,
    The kind where every man can dream of fun and sex.
    (*Winking*) Glamour girls bursting in their upper decks . . .

(Out of the Dream Machine bursts an actress dressed as MARILYN MONROE *speaking, dancing and singing in what Norman Mailer calls her "sweet little rinky-dink of a voice with all the cleanliness of all the clean American backyards.")*

MARILYN MONROE:
Cameras laugh as my breasts
Fly out of my dress.
Who sleeps when fame strips you naked?
You reach for sleeping pills
When Old Man Insomnia kills ...

(Singing refrain as the NARRATOR *joins her in a dream-like dance and song-duet.*

Fame will go by ...
And, so long,
I've had you, Fame ...

Mr. Boss shouts at me *Finished! Always late!*
Mr. Coroner numbers me *eighty-one, one, two, eight—*
Fame's number in a numbered time.
A sex symbol becomes a thing
And a thing cannot sing ...

(Refrain with NARRATOR*)*

Fame will go by ...
And, so long,
I've had you, Fame ...

MARILYN MONROE:
Alone in my room I say
"Make it dark and give me air."
You've got to open the dark to dream,
But the lonely are always late,
The lonely have another date ...

(Refrain with NARRATOR*)*

Fame will go by ...
And, so long,
I've had you, Fame ...

(After a turn with the NARRATOR *she exits with her wriggling dance, singing her refrain and waving, as the* NARRATOR *waves goodbye.)*

NARRATOR: (*Stepping towards her, holding out his hand to his dream of Marilyn*)

    Dead... In the dark love flows away
    And we learn to live another day...
    If we can't have love, we call for Wealth, Fame...
    On top of the heap we look out far
    For the King of the Mountain, an American star...
    High up there he glares, an eagle in flight,
    Ends hunched over his tapes lost in the night,
    Alone in his house where the frontier ends,
    Writing his memoirs as the dark descends...

KING OF THE MOUNTAIN:

(*He wears a Nixon mask. As he sits listening to his tape recorder he hears his voice echoing eerily on tape. Sometimes he repeats part of the taped phrases in a strange counterpoint.*)

All I wanted was the lift of a driving dream...

(*The tape echoes "lift of a driving dream...lift of a dri—ving dream"...*)

Bee—trayed...Snake tapes... Those kids betrayed me... They threw mudballs at the White House at every opportunity... They wanted a red America...Never!...

(*the tape echoes "A red America—Never"...He mouths the word "Never", looks angrily at the tape recorder, pokes it.*)

Snake tapes... Who would have thought the old tapes would proliferate?... Why didn't I burn the tapes?

(*The tape echoes, "Why didn't I burn the tapes?"*)

How can you burn History when you've created it?...For the first time in man's history I had it in my hands—to record power accurately...Catch every little detail of power for the first time...

(*The tape echoes, "Every little detail for the first time"...*)

King of the Mountain, that's what they called me!

(*The tape echoes "King of the Mountain... King of the Mountain" as he mouths the words.*)

Beee—trayed!...Do they want to pick my carcass?... I'm not a skeleton yet...My writing will vindicate me...

3

KING OF THE MOUNTAIN CONT'D

> (*He pats the MSS near him.*) Vin—di—cate me!...(*Looking up*) Sky...Space...Moon...Beau—ti—ful---My name... American names on the moon...*Moooon*...In *my* time...
>
> (*The tape echoes* 'Moooon...*In* my *time*"...)
>
> I did my best... *My* best... My *best*... In the best interests of the nation... Naaa—tion... Some mistakes... *Miss—takes*... Errors of judgment...
>
> (*The tape echoes* "Miss—takes... Errors of Judgment"...)
>
> *Those bastards*... My advisers... I thought they'd throw themselves on a damn sword for me...
>
> (*The tape echoes* "Throw themselves on a damn sword for me"...)
>
> *Those idiots with their domestic capers*... Writing their spy stories... Their thrillers... They want to put my head in a cage... They want to put me on display in the papers... X-ray me on television... Media disease... *Me—di—a dis—ease*...
>
> (*The tape echoes* "Media disease... Me—di—a dis—ease"...)
>
> *Cri—sis*... That's greatness... Hang in there... Throw the long bomb if necessary... No one else could decide... So many votes I got... They all loved me... My great game plan... I can still hear them applauding... I raise my arms...
>
> (*He raises his arms in his victory stance.*)

VOICES: (*Echoing on tape as he mouths the words*)

> When the going gets tough, the tough get going..
> When the tough get going, the going gets tough...
> When the going gets going, the going gets tough...
> When the going gets tough, the going gets going...
> When the tough get going, the tough get going...
> When the going gets tough, the tough get going...

KING OF THE MOUNTAIN:

> *Beeee—traaaayed*... You bastard kids... We never conceived you... All you kids can do is say your filthy words in public... At least I had the decency to say them on secret tapes... How would you bastard children understand the mystery of hidden swearwords?... You kids shit on language, that's all you do... All your god damn demonstrations lost in time... You don't have me to kick around anymore...

KING OF THE MOUNTAIN CONT'D

> (*The tape echoes "lost in time . . . You don't have me to kick around anymore"...*)

In time it will all come clear . . . My real game plan . . . To turn the earth into a game for all mankind . . . A peace game . . . A generation of peace . . .

> (*The tape echoes "A game for all mankind . . . A peace game . . . A generation of peace"...*)

Jeee—sus . . . No escape . . . *Beee—trayed* . . . Hidden tape recorders . . . My players couldn't even follow the script . . .

> (*Shouting at the tape recorder*) Go on, pick my carcass . . . I was King of the Mountain . . . Your voices will die in time . . . I have my pardon . . . Publishers will pay me millions for my story . . . I'll write my story . . . Millions will read it . . . Translated all over the world . . . I'll be redeemed . . . *Re—deemed* . . .

> (*The tape echoes "Redeemed . . . Re—deemed"...*)

Defiance then . . . Farewell to false voices . . . (*He turns off the tape recorder.*) *De—fi—ance* . . . King of the Mountain . . . My old stance . . . Against the world . . .

> (*Slowly he fades back into the Dream Machine as the* NARRATOR *steps forward again.*)

NARRATOR: (*Staring at the machine*)

Be careful with this machine . . . Sometimes it speaks
Its own mind, wanders, races, leaks
What it pleases as is the way of dreams
When fact and fancy flow together in their streams . . .

> (*Looking at the machine a little apprehensively*)

Tonight we hope it's programmed properly
To enter the dream-world where we learn to see . . .

> (*The Dream Machine begins to work mysteriously.*)

With our machine's modern computer device
We conjure up a vast Cathedral of Ice . . .

> (*Light changes to indicate the Cathedral of Ice.*)

We'll search with you how dreams of power
Linger on today to haunt each waking hour . . .

> (*More lighting changes to intensify the effect of the Cathedral of Ice.*)

NARRATOR CONT'D

Now for our play excuse me, please.
Like all of us, my dreams must change
As I become Dream-Fuehrer, power to arrange...

(*He puts on a mustache, brushes his hair over his forehead, and becomes* HITLER.)

(*As the* NARRATOR *transforms himself into* HITLER, *the Dream Machine lights up with appropriate illumination.*)

HITLER: (*exuberantly*)

I'm your Dream-Fuehrer. Laugh, cry with me, Ladies and gentlemen. Here in my Cathedral of Ice the dreams of power never die. What you hate by day you love at night. Against your enemies your Dream-Fuehrer is a rainbow of hope.

(*He gestures and a large photographic image of* HITLER *as a knight in armor is projected on a screen above the Machine.*)

Laugh, ladies and gentlemen, laugh at your Dream-Fuehrer. Laugh at the Dream-Fuehrer's wife...

(EVA BRAUN *makes her dream-like appearance out of the Dream Machine singing "Tea for Two" as she sang it in the bunker the night before she died.*)

HITLER: (*cutting her off after a time*)

That's enough Eva. You sang that song just before we died. You sing it too much.

EVA: (*stopping obediently*) Yes, Adolf.

HITLER: (*continuing to the audience*)

Through laughter, through song, we begin to feel the power of the will, how Dream-Fuehrers conquer even in defeat. You think my toothbrush mustache an accident? My dangling forelock happened by chance? Pure dream images. Napoleon was almost midget-short, so small that he created a dream-stance of power for eternity...

(HITLER *motions and in a niche, as if out of the Dream Machine, the figure of Napoleon appears. He is seated on the imperial throne as if in Ingres's famous "Portrait of Napoleon I on His Imperial Throne" (1806). In addition to his imperial robe and crown, he holds the Hand of Justice and wears the sword of Charlemagne.*)

EVA: (*gaping, impressed*) Look, Adolf, you've brought back Napoleon.

HITLER:
> On his throne when he became Emperor Napoleon the First. You see his sword and the Hand of Justice he holds? They belonged to Charlemagne.

EVA: Really? Charlemagne?

HITLER:
> Yes, Napoleon was the imperial successor to the Holy Roman Empire, the first leader before me to unify Europe. I'll tell you a secret, Eva. I always wanted to die on May 5, the same day Napoleon died...

NAPOLEON: (*sharply*)
> You died on April 30, six days before my death.

HITLER:
> The German people betrayed me. They couldn't hold Berlin.

NAPOLEON:
> You should never have invaded Russia.

HITLER: (*sarcastically*)
> You're an authority, of course...
> What happened to your artillery in the snow?

NAPOLEON:
> The winter was abnormally severe. You should have known your heavy tanks would get stuck in the ice. Anyway I reached Moscow. You never reached Moscow.

HITLER:
> I conquered the Ukraine. If Goering hadn't ruined the Luftwaffe I would have triumphed before winter set in. Next time we should strike the Ukraine again.

NAPOLEON:
> Nonsense, you went too far south. Next time we must have a frontal attack on Moscow the way I planned.

HITLER: (*shouting at* Napoleon)
> History has taught you nothing. I'll show you. I'll prove to the world man becomes great through dream-conquests. Struggle is the father of all things. Virtue lies in blood. Leadership is primary and decisive...

EVA: (*tugging at his sleeve*) That's one of your old speeches, Adolf . . .

HITLER: (*as* NAPOLEON *fades away*)

    Napoleon will have to learn if he's going to remain a real Dream-Fuehrer . . .

    (*Actors as* STALIN, ROOSEVELT, CHURCHILL, *perhaps in masks, are seen in an eerie, dream-like "Yalta Dance," perhaps around a round table, as they shake hands formally, push* ROOSEVELT *around in his wheel chair, etc.*)

EVA: (*gaping again*) Look . . . Your enemies . . .

HITLER:

    Don't worry . . . Only fading dream-figures . . . Stalin, Roosevelt, Churchill in their Yalta dance . . .

EVA: (*smiling*) Their Yalta dance?

HITLER:

    Yes, those dreamers thought they could divide Europe. Stalin tricked them. I'll defeat them all in time. They won't get into my Cathedral of Ice . . .

    (*The dream-figures of Stalin, Roosevelt, and Churchill fade away.*)

EVA: (*excitedly*) They're gone? Adolf, you *are* Dream-Fuehrer . . .

HITLER: (*complacently*)

    Out of my Dream-Apparatus I continue to create my Third Reich. In our dreams we begin to discover ourselves, escape from our parents . . .

    (*Something explodes in the Dream Machine and two performers dressed like Hitler's parents appear.*)

EVA: (*nudging* HITLER *as his back is turned*)

    Adolf, I don't think you've escaped . . .

HITLER'S FATHER: (*He speaks his Customs Official title twice, sharply, as if correcting his wife and son, reminding them of his position, then bows stiffly.*)

EVA: Is that your father?

HITLER:

    Don't worry about him. He's just a ghost. He was a man who wanted only to be respectable.

MOTHER: (*impatiently to the Father*) Uncle Alois, Uncle Alois ...

EVA: What's she saying?

HITLER: My mother always called my father, "Uncle Alois."

    (*Eva breaks into laughter.*)

    Even in the bedroom she called him "Uncle Alois."

FATHER: (*calling sharply*) You never respected my uniform.

HITLER:
    Your uniform never meant anything. The uniform of a minor Austrian Customs Official, that's all.

MOTHER: (*protesting*) You should respect your father, Adolf.

HITLER:
    Poor little tyrant. What does that ghost know about real power? His uniform only obscured the dreams of authority that he tried to enforce on me.

FATHER: (*calling his title again sharply and dogmatically*)

MOTHER: (*alarmed as they begin to fade away in the Apparatus for Dreams*)

    Uncle Alois, Uncle Alois ... He's the Fuehrer!

HITLER: (*impatiently as they disappear into the Dream Machine*)

    No one thinks of my parents any more. Lost in their bourgeois roles, they left me to become the real dreamer. They sentenced me to school where more bourgeois authorities tried to confine me ...

    (*An old, grim-looking provincial Austrian school-teacher appears dimly, in dim light as if struggling vainly to become a real dream. He is waving a pointer menacingly at* HITLER.)

All those provincial Austrian schoolteachers could do was induce boredom as they waved their pointers at me over some bit of nonsense. My first report card was so bad I got drunk, tore it up, and used it for toilet paper ...

EVA: (*laughing*) You didn't!

    (*The Dream-Teacher holds up a torn report card and waves the pointer menacingly at* HITLER *who smiles and waves him back into the Apparatus for Dreams.*)

HITLER:
> Goodbye to school. Lessons of power are learned in the streets. Today every new Dream Machine adds to the power of the Dream-Fuehrer. (*gesturing at the Apparatus*) Look carefully, ladies and gentlemen, out of my Dream Machine I continue to shape my Cathedral of Ice for the future...
>
> (*The unpredictable Dream Machine explodes again and* NEUMANN *steps out of it with the Jewish coat...*)

NEUMANN: And the past, Fuehrer. Don't forget the past.

HITLER: Neumann... You don't belong here.

NEUMANN: You can't eliminate every little man so easily.

HITLER: Get out of my dreams.

NEUMANN: (*smiling*)
> I wish I could. I brought your Jewish coat. You'll need it to keep warm in the Cathedral of Ice.

EVA: (*nudging* HITLER)
> Who is that old man? What's he mean by Jewish coat?

HITLER: (*ignoring her, to* NEUMANN)
> I don't need your filthy old coat anymore. It was long ago in Vienna, when I was a poor student, I bought it from you. You tried to swindle me, you Jewish peddler.

NEUMANN: I gave it to you. I did your business. We lived in the same poorhouse.

HITLER: You never gave away anything. I'll build my Cathedral without Rome, without Jews.

NEUMANN: I sold your painted postcards, gave you money to live on. You'll need your coat...

HITLER: All you sell is filth. I cleaned up Vienna. I got rid of you, Neumann. You're dead, you and all your disgraceful Jewish whores spreading their syphilis...
> (*Mockingly* NEUMANN *begins to sell* HITLER'S *postcards while Three Whores of Vienna like satirical, antagonistic ghosts sing "The Ballad of the Jewish Whores of Vienna."*)

THE JEWISH WHORES: (*singing*)

> That's what we do
> From dusk until dawn
> We infect with disgrace
> All the Aryan race—
> We're the Great Jewish Whores of Vienna...

HITLER: (*shouting at them*):

> Out of my Cathedral of Ice! Out! You attack everyone with syphilis...

EVA: (*plucking at his sleeve,*) Syphilis, Adolf, syphilis...

THE JEWISH WHORES: (*singing*)

> That's what we do
> From dusk until dawn—
> We attack, we attack
> Though flat on our back—
> We're the Great Jewish Whores of Vienna...

HITLER: (*raving at them*):

> You're dead, you Jewish whores. Only one thing triumphs, terror and force...

THE JEWISH WHORES: (*singing*)

> That's what we do
> From dusk until dawn—
> We use terror and force
> And show no remorse—
> We're the Great Jewish Whores of Vienna...

> (*Laughing they drop their roles as Whore and return to their positions as observers in the Cathedral of Ice.* NEUMANN *continues to sell* HITLER'S *painted postcards*)

NEUMANN:

> Postcards for sale... Little painted postcards by Adolf Hitler... Rare reproductions... Pictures of famous Viennese monuments... All by Adolf Hitler... Reduced prices...

EVA: You shouldn't let him sell your work so cheaply, Adolf...

HITLER: Stop selling my work cheaply, Neumann. It's worth much more today.

NEUMANN: (*continuing his pitch to the audience*)

> Come buy, ladies and gentlemen...Remember the Inflation... Get your little painted postcards...The Little painted postcards of Adolf Hitler...

HITLER: (*proudly*)

> They're worth a fortune now, my postcards...I'm a better painter than Winston Churchill...Come here, Neumann.

NEUMANN: (*approaching mockingly*) Yes, Fuehrer...What is your wish?

HITLER: Take back your Jewish coat.

NEUMANN: It's cold in the Cathedral of Ice...My coat will help.

HITLER: It's got lice in it.

NEUMANN: What do you expect from a Vienna poor-house?

HITLER:

> You know how I hated that poor-house, but I always kept my clothes clean. You gave me a dirty coat.

NEUMANN: You were glad enough to wear it...

HITLER:

> I never wanted your Jewish coat...That miserable city of lotus-eaters was five years of shame for me...

NEUMANN: (*smiling*)

> We Jews lotus-eaters? If there were any food to induce forgetfulness we'd eat it...

HITLER:

> You tried to be a good Jew and seduce me with your coat. But you hid your money like the rest of them

NEUMANN: (*shrugging*)

> What money? If you find yourself tied to a Hitler who needs money?

EVA: Get him to sell something else. That's all he's good for.

HITLER: (*producing a box of campaign ribbons out of the Dream Machine*)

> Why don't you sell my campaign ribbons?... It's time to remember my great victories...(*As Neumann only smiles,* HITLER

HITLER CONT'D
> *starts hawking the ribbons & medals*) Poland, 1939 . . . France, 1940, my greatest triumph . . . Belgium, Holland . . . Norway, Finland, Denmark, the Scandinavian countries . . . An endless list . . . All of Europe . . . North Africa . . . Greece, Yugoslavia . . . Come, ladies and gentlemen, help me build my Cathedral of Ice . . . What will you give me for my great Russian Campaign Medal?
>
> *(He starts to shiver as the Apparatus begins to ice over with a chill)*
>
> Turn up the heat . . . It's cold in here . . .
>
> (NEUMANN *helps him put on the coat*)
>
> That damn Russian winter killed my troops . . . Why don't you sell some real souvenirs? . . . *(with increasing frenzy)* Sell them my new weapons . . . The military powers need my buzz-bombs, my rockets, my new jet planes, my tanks . . . If you want a real souvenir, sell them my Mercedes touring car . . .

SCHRECK: *(shooting angrily out of the Dream Machine)*
> You can't sell the Mercedes . . . It was my car too . . . I drove it, I polished it, I cared for it until you spoiled everything . . .

EVA: *(delighted to see* SCHRECK, *although he ignores her)*
> Adolf, it's Schreck, your chauffeur. He's come to drive us to Berchtesgaden. We'll have some fun . . .

HITLER: Schreck, we had good times together. How can you say I spoiled everything?

SCHRECK: *(doggedly like a child)* You forbade me to drive fast anymore . . .

HITLER: We couldn't run down every peasant who came out to cheer me.

GOERING: *(appearing in the Dream Machine, waving a cigar)*
> Forget him, Fuehrer. He's only a chauffeur. We don't need him in the Cathedral of Ice.

HITLER: *(raging)* You don't know who we need. I decide who lives here.

GOERING: I committed suicide for you at Nuernberg.

HITLER: *(gesturing with contempt at* GOERING'S *cigar)*
> You know I hate smoking . . . How many times do I have to tell you you can't be represented in a historical monument smoking a cigar . . .

(GOERING *shrugs, continues to smoke his cigar, watching.*)

HITLER: (*cryng out, summoning the* ARCHITECT) Where's my Architect?...

(*The* ARCHITECT *appears and walks to Hitler.*)

This Architect is mine. He draws the plans for my new world. Every drawing is corrected by my pen...

(*He tugs at his coat and says to the* ARCHITECT)

You want my Jewish coat from Vienna? I can't . . . can't get it off...

(*The* ARCHITECT *moves to help him and he thrusts the* ARCHITECT *away.*)

Get away . . . You're useless. If you're my Architect why can't you design me a real home?

ARCHITECT: Yes, Fuehrer, what style would you like?

HITLER:

Like my old home at Obersalzberg, the only place where I could relax . . . That's what they want to see in the Cathedral of Ice...

EVA: Let's go to Obersalzberg... We had the most fun there...

ARCHITECT: Yes, Fuehrer... (*calling*)

The Procession to the Teahouse at Berchtesgaden...

(*He signals and a procession forms on the ramp that represents the curving mountain walk to the teahouse at Obersalzberg.*)

HITLER:

That's right . . . For once you've got the right idea . . . The walk to the Teahouse is my favorite walk...

(*On the ramp two security men lead the procession. Everyone in this scene is dressed in civilian clothes so at first the the gayety of the walk dominates. After the initial humorous confusion, the rigidity of the nightmare-like ritualistic walk becomes apparent.*)

ARCHITECT: (*near the foot of the ramp*)

If anyone is Hitler's friend I am his friend . . . So I always have to accompany him . . . The path up the mountain to the

ARCHITECT CONT'D
>teahouse is narrow . . . Room for ony two abreast . . . Two security men lead the procession . . .
>
>> (*Mechanically the security men start up the path*)
>
>Then comes Hitler talking to his immediate favorite . . .
>
>> (HITLER *starts up the path talking genially to a man. Two other members of the walking group appear. The rear of the procession is brought up by a female secretary and* EVA BRAUN.)
>
>At the procession's end march his secretary and his mistress Eva Braun . . .

EVA BRAUN: (*correcting him*) I'm his wife now . . .

ARCHITECT: (*continuing as a dog barks*) His police dog darts about . . .

HITLER: (*calls sharply, shrugs when the dog fails to appear*)
>Here, Blondi . . . Here Blondi . . . Blondi . . .
>
>> (HITLER *turns, summons another favorite, which causes a frantic, abrupt adjustment in the order of the procession.*)

HITLER:
>No, no, you've got it all wrong . . . Can't you remember the way it went?

ARCHITECT: (*at the rear of the procession now*)
>Every German wonder that I learned as a boy hangs in the air over this walk . . . If only the Fuehrer will summon me again to be a great architect . . . For the commission to design an important building I'll sell my soul . . .
>
>> (*The ritualistic walk begins again revealing its increasingly mechanical, servile nature. Suddenly* HITLER *turns, beckons impatiently to the* ARCHITECT, *who jumps to the Fuehrer's side. The* ARCHITECT *assumes the favored position beside* HITLER *and behind the security men in the procession.*)

HITLER: How do you like the Obersalzberg?

ARCHITECT: Magnificent . . .

HITLER: Here I spend the finest hours of my life . . . (*He calls to his dog again*) Blondi! (*then affectionately*) That dog never minds me . . . (*sharply*) He's the only one . . .

ARCHITECT: It is a beautiful view.

HITLER: (*musing*)
> All my great projects are conceived and ripened in these mountains... (*he points*) You see the Untersberg?

ARCHITECT: (*staring*) Lovely.

HITLER: (*sharply*) The Emperor Charlemagne sleeps there.
> (*Reverently emphasizing the legend to the* ARCHITECT)
>
> You remember the legend, "When he arises the past glory of the German Empire will be restored."... Hear me Emperor Charlemagne... In your tomb do you hear me?... (*The cast echoes the sound of "Charlemagne."*) Germany is finished with play-acting. No longer will Germany be betrayed by Jews and bourgeois democrats. Hear me, Charlemagne! (*The cast echoes "Charlemagne" again*) I pledge you a new German empire. My troops will march again through the streets of Europe. Rise from your tomb... Hand in hand we'll walk across the map of Europe... Charlemagne!... We'll rule together in the Cathedral of Ice!
>
> (*The entire cast sings the "Ballad of the Cathedral of Ice"*)

HITLER:
> Charlemagne!
> Rise from your tomb.
> Dreams have no price.
> Power lives on
> In my Cathedral of Ice...

CAST:
> Charlemagne!
> Come buy your joy or sorrow.
> In the Cathedral of Ice
> We freeze you for tomorrow.

HITLER:
> Charlemagne!
> I pledge you a new Empire,
> A new Aryan race
> Out of blood, war, fire!

CAST:
> Charlemagne!
> Come buy your joy or sorrow.
> In the Cathedral of Ice
> We freeze you for tomorrow.

HITLER: Charlemagne!
 Into history, into time,
 Our troops march on
 Forever into dream.

CAST: Charlemagne!
 Come buy your joy or sorrow.
 In the Cathedral of Ice
 We freeze you for tomorrow . . .

(*Slowly, costumed like a kind of 19th century Wagnerian reincarnation of medieval power, the dream-figure of Charlemagne rises from his tomb in the Dream Machine and dances a little jig of power with* HITLER *as the cast sings the final refrain.*)

Scene 2 — Hitler's Children

(*After Charlemagne disappears back into his tomb,* HITLER *signals in frenzied exultation and a large Nazi flag drops down.*)

HITLER:
 At last our Dream Machine is working perfectly. Here, with my favorite Architect (*a gesture to the* ARCHITECT), we create for eternity our famous German ruins. We freeze all traitors, Jews, into the ice-walls of our national fortress. (*to the* ARCHITECT) Invite them to meet my children.

ARCHITECT: (*to audience*)
 Ladies and gentlemen, we invite you to meet Hitler's children . . .
 (*A corner of the flag is drawn up and we see the beginning of the line of children wavering uncertainly in time*)

HITLER: (*interrupting*)
 No, let me speak first . . . I'll put my children in the right perspective . . .
 (*As* HITLER *steps up on a platform to start the introduction of his "children", the flag is raised higher and the full line of children is revealed.*)

HITLER:
> How petty are the thoughts of small men. I always aim at something a thousand times higher. I want to become the destroyer of Marxism. I am still going to achieve this task. I will destroy Communism throughout the world! When I stood for the first time at the grave of Richard Wagner, my heart overflowed with pride in his genius. He had forbidden the usual sort of flowery inscription such as *Here Lies His Excellency, Baron Richard Von Wagner.* He gave himself to the world without any titles of vanity. I am proud to follow in his footsteps. The man who is born to be a dictator is not forced into it. His will triumphs. There is nothing immodest about this. Is it immodest for a worker to drive himself to heavy labor? Is it presumptuous for a thinker to ponder through the nights until he gives the world a great invention? The man who is called upon to govern has no right to say, "If you summon me I will cooperate." No, it is his duty to step forward even through death.
>
> (HITLER *steps forward. His children cry "Sieg Heil!" three times.*)

HITLER: (*smiling to the* ARCHITECT *with satisfaction*)
> Come forward my children . . . Behave yourselves . . .
>
> (*At the head of the line* GOEBBELS *steps forward to celebrate* HITLER. *While* GOEBBELS *speaks* HITLER *listens, nodding with satisfaction, occasionally slapping the short whip that he carries against his coat.*)

GOEBBELS:
> Like a rising star before our wondering eyes you appear . . . You perform miracles to clear our minds . . . You speak the greatest words Germany has heard since Bismarck . . . You unify the Great German Reich, purify it for eternity . . . You name the need of a new generation . . . We thank you . . . Europe and the world will thank you . . .

HITLER: (*to* GOEBBELS)
> A good speaker . . . That's why you're my propaganda minister . . . You're faithful. But I had to teach you a lesson. In power you can't trust anyone. Remember what you called me once at an early Party meeting?

GOEBBELS: (*forced to recall a nightmare*)

I demand that the petty bourgeois, Adolf Hitler, be expelled from the Nazi Party for accepting favors and privileges from the wealthy! (*hysterically*) Can't you ever forget?

HITLER: A dictator never forgets his bastard children. You went to college too much. Eight universities, wasn't it?

GOEBBELS: Yes.

HITLER: You confused your mind with too many subjects—history, philosophy, literature, art, Latin, Greek...You wrote bad plays, a poor autobiographical novel...

GOEBBELS: (*agreeing reluctantly*)

It was a terrible novel...(*under his breath*) You weren't a good painter either.

HITLER: (*shouting*) What's that?...(GOEBBELS *mutters, "Nothing."*)

The important thing is I taught you how to use the arts for political power.

GOEBBELS: You taught me everything.

HITLER: Not quite. Your crippled foot . . . You still want to climb into bed with every little actress you can find just to assert your masculinity...

GOEBBELS: (*spitting out venomously*)

My limp kept me chained to a desk, walking lopsided, a dwarf of history...

HITLER: (*gesturing with his whip*)

Without your limp you're nothing. It gives you the instinct of hatred...

GOEBBELS: Yes...

HITLER: (*tapping his leg with his whip*)

A touch of hatred gives a man a mysterious quality...

GOEBBELS: You've always been the mysterious Fuehrer to me.

HITLER: (*smiling a little, now that he's humiliated* GOEBBELS)

> My problem is still to give my Hakenkreuz, my swastika, a new dramatic mystery. I want it to strike the eye of even the most simple-minded person.

GOEBBELS: Your design remains an inspiration to us all . . .

HITLER: (*pointing to the flag*)

> In red I see my war against communism. In white the cause of nationalism. And in the swastika the final victory of Aryan man. Stand aside, Joseph . . . Let's see the rest of my children.
>
> > (HITLER *pokes up the corner of the flag a little more with his whip and looks down the line of "children" as if to make sure of their appearance and obedience in the Cathedral of Ice.*)

HITLER:

> What simple creatures. You'll never sell me out to the peace-mongers, eh? A strong party needs men like you . . .

GOEBBELS: (*wide-eyed with reverence*)

> Only such men can conquer the bourgeoisie . . .

HITLER: (*nodding assent*)

> If a bourgeois gives me a hundred marks he thinks he's given me all of Bavaria. But these men, what sacrifices they're willing to make . . . All day at their jobs . . . All night off on a mission for the Party.
>
> (*They nod assent in their distinctively crude ways.*)
>
> Especially I look for men a little rough in appearance. When they walk into a hall people sit up. A bourgeois in a stiff collar ruins everything.

GOEBBELS: (*eagerly*)

> As a favor may I introduce them, Fuehrer?

HITLER: (*as if granting a favor to a child*)

> If you wish. Let's have Schreck first. I'm going to need him again.

GOEBBELS: (*announcing*)

> Julius Schreck, private chauffeur and bodyguard to the Fuehrer . . .

(*As they pretend to drive through history with* SCHRECK *at the wheel, the cast joins in "The Ballad of the German Motorists."*)

CAST: (*singing*)

> We're motorists of Germany,
> Inventors of the People's Car,
> So small and cheap that anyone
> Can buy a bug to ride in fun.

SCHRECK: (*speaking*) Have you bought your People's Car?

CAST: (*singing refrain*)

> Volkswagen, Volkswagen...
> We'll drive from Berlin to Cannes
> On the Autobahn, Autobahn...

CAST: (*singing*)

> We're the motorists of Germany,
> Creators of the fast sports car,
> Building free the Autobahn
> To speed forever on and on...

SCHRECK: (*speaking*) Have you bought your fast sports car?

CAST: (*singing refrain*)

> Porsche, Porsche...
> We'll drive from Berlin to Cannes
> On the Autobahn, Autobahn...

CAST: (*singing*)

> We're motorists of Germany,
> Designers of the new sedan—
> We seat your family on a throne
> Of power where you rule alone...

SCHRECK: (*speaking*) Come buy your family a sedan!

CAST: (*singing refrain*)

> Mercedes, Mercedes...
> We'll drive from Berlin to Cannes
> On the Autobahn, Autobahn!

SCHRECK: (*with sudden bitterness, pleading to* HITLER)

> Can I drive fast again?

HITLER: (*impatiently*) Soon, soon . . .

SCHRECK: (*possessed, he won't be put off*)

> I'm a great driver. I could have been Germany's number one race driver. In our supercharged Mercedes we used to pass all the American cars. We'd force them to the side of the road . . .

HITLER: (*remembering pleasantly*)

> American cars were nothing compared to a Mercedes. Their motors would overheat. They'd pull over with steam pouring out of their radiators. What fun . . .

SCHRECK: (*shouting*)

> Then you ordered me not to drive over fifty. Me, a great driver!

HITLER: (*annoyed*)

> Poor simple Schreck . . . You won't learn . . . You have the vision of a great driver, but no sense of public destiny. I created Volkswagen, Porsche, and Mercedes . . . They owe everything to me . . .
>
> (*Impatiently he waves* SCHRECK *off with his whip and motions* GOEBBELS *to continue with the introductions.*)

GOEBBELS: (*announcing with glee*)

> Heinrich Hoffman, your official photographer . . .
>
> (EVA BRAUN, *disguised as Hoffman, steps forward and snaps pictures of* HITLER *as he poses smiling in his new role of power.*)

HITLER: (*as he poses*)

> Heinrich, you're a man who knows the camera's power. As a photographer you're always in the background at the right time. You can still help me along with the right photographs . . . And you introduced me to Eva Braun when she worked for you, eh, Heinrich?

EVA: (*taking off her hat and grinning at* HITLER) Yes, Adolf.

HITLER: (*laughing with delight*)

> Eva, you rascal. You always play games on me. Go on now . . . You're holding up my children.
>
> (*She laughs, snaps another photo, and runs off.*)

(*A weird figure emerges grimly from the line of children. He struggles futilely to speak through time. It is* ERNST ROEHM *trying to redeem his place in history. He struggles furiously to push his way forward as the bully-boys try to keep him back in line.*)

ROEHM: I demand to be heard . . . I'm your old comrade . . . My only wish is to be a soldier for the Third Reich . . .

HITLER: (*hysterically*)

How did he get into my Cathedral of Ice? (*to* GOEBBELS) I don't permit traitors here. (*turning on* ROEHM) Ernst Roehm, traitor, that's your name. I had you shot . . .

GOEBBELS: (*groveling*) He won't die . . .

ROEHM: (*struggling with the bully-boys*)

There is some error, Adolf . . . If you want to kill me why don't you do it yourself?

HITLER: (*screaming*)

Don't call me Adolf. No one calls me by my first name. I am the Fuehrer . . .

GOEBBELS: (*trying desparately to placate* HITLER)

Touch him with your whip, Fuehrer. Make him disappear in time.

HITLER: (*lashing out with his whip*)

Back to your death, Roehm. Tell your story to the grave . . . No one listens to your lies. The Fuehrer stands alone in history . . .

(*He takes a defiant stance of loneliness beneath the swastika.*)

GOEBBELS: (*cautiously after the bully-boys seem to have subdued* ROEHM)

Shall I go on, Fuehrer? . . .

HITLER: (*shaking suspiciously again*) Is Roehm silent? . . .

GOEBBELS: (*soothingly*)

Yes, I'm sure he won't be any more trouble . . . The next is Rudolf Hess, your loyal secretary . . .

(HESS *steps forward, pleased, slightly bewildered, mad in time. He recites like a schoolboy from his prizewinning essay at the University of Munich, "What Will The Man Be Like Who Will Lead Germany Back To Her Old Grandeur?"*)

HESS: (*reciting*)

Where all authority has vanished only a man of the people can restore authority. The deeper the dictator is rooted in the masses, the better he understands them psychologically . . .

HITLER: (*as if nodding encouragement to a child*)

Very good, Rudolf. You're better as a student . . .

HESS: (*continuing with new confidence*)

Like every great man the dictator is all personality. When necessity commands he does not shrink from bloodshed. Great questions are always decided by blood and iron. In order to reach his goal he is prepared to trample on his closest friends . . .

HITLER: (*impatiently*)

That's a lie. Too bad you lost your mind . . . Your crazy flight to England . . . You should have crashed in the British Channel.

(*With his whip he motions* HESS *back into line.*)

GOEBBELS: (*maliciously, enjoying the next encounter*)

Hermann Goering, fat man, drug addict . . .

GOERING: (*He is clad in elements of a once-glorious hunting costume, hat, shorts, colorful high stockings, leather vest, dagger at his waist. Immediately he attacks* GOEBBELS.)

Shut up you crippled dwarf . . . I answer only to the Fuehrer . . .

GOEBBELS: (*taunting him*) Is that why you're so far back in line? . . .

HITLER : (*in a tirade to* GOERING)

We don't need your ridiculous hunting costume here. Killing animals, if one must eat meat, is the butcher's business. To dress up in ridiculous costumes might be all right if you used a bow and arrow, but all you use is a fat belly and a gun . . .

GOERING: (*unhearing, enthusiastic, remembering as if in a dream*)

I bagged a buck . . . He was drinking at a stream when we

GOEBBELS CONT'D

    spotted him from the ridge above ... Then he caught wind of us and bolted halfway up the mountain ...

HITLER: (*annoyed*)

    I don't want to hear about your hunting. We have important business.

GOERING: Is anything wrong?

HITLER: I want you to spend less time on hunting and devote yourself more to our transit problems.

GOERING: (*slowly*) Cars and highways? But the Luftwaffe ...

HITLER: I want Autobahns everywhere. Everyone should have his Volkswagen.

GOEBBELS: (*jumping in smoothly*)

    We can make the newspapers print special sections on the pleasures of traveling by car.

HITLER: Excellent ... That's the kind of action I want. (*to* GOERING) What do you think?

GOERING: (*carefully*)

    We must consider carefully. The Air Force must be our first effort ...

HITLER: (*raging*)

    You're ruining the Luftwaffe ... You're a drug addict ... Hard drugs ... Heroin ... I won't have it.

    (GOERING *shrugs and turns back into line.*)

GOEBBELS: (*enjoying* GOERING'S *put-down*)

    Heinrich Himmler, head of the SS and the Gestapo ...

HIMMLER: (*stepping forward, tight-lipped*)

    Fuehrer, everything we discussed about the camps was strictly in privacy.

HITLER: You can't keep your mouth shut ... A small poultry farmer, that's all you are, Heinrich ... You have the simple mind of a clerk. Somehow you became the most-feared man in the world. By hating you they love me. That's why I keep you around ...

HIMMLER: (*saluting*)

> Ja, mein Fuehrer...(*He steps back into line*)

GOEBBELS: (*pointing to the line*)

> Should be bother with the bully-boys?

HITLER: One or two if you wish...

GOEBBELS:

> They go quickly...Julius Streicher, Party Leader of Franconia, newspaper editor...(STREICHER *steps out warily*)

HITLER: (*angrily*)

> Julius Pornographer...We don't want him...(*to* STREICHER) You keep a camera in the ceiling over your bed to record your sexual escapades...

STREICHER: (*protesting*)

> I'm your strongest supporter...I call you by your first name, Adolf...

HITLER:

> A privilege you never deserved...You should use your whip like a lion-tamer. You only use it for your private sadism... (*And he lashes* STREICHER *back into line*)

GOEBBELS: (*continuing hastily to appease* HITLER'S *wrath*))

> Ulrich Graf, your bodyguard...Butcher's apprentice, amateur wrestler...

HITLER: (*with satisfaction, inspecting Graf's muscles*)

> A good bodyguard. You like to fight. Great physical strength...At party meetings you can be useful in throwing out troublemakers. (*He pats* GRAF'S *arm, patting him back into line*) That's enough children, Joseph...

GOEBBELS: Yes, my Fuehrer...

HITLER: Let them entertain me.

> (GOEBBELS *and the* CHILDREN *sing* "*The Big Lie.*" HITLER *stands with the* ARCHITECT *beneath swastika, beating time with his whip. The archaic, dignified figure of* KARL MAY, *dressed in formal civilian clothes of around 1900, appears upstage behind the* CHILDREN *during the song, waiting impatiently to address* HITLER.)

Song of the Big Lie

THE CHILDREN: (*singing*)

    Tell the Big Lie—
    It's the Truth,
    It's the Truth
      if it's told
        long enough...

GOEBBELS: (*singing the refrain*)

    Big Lies will bring you triumph sweet
    If you repeat, repeat, repeat...

ALL: (*echoing*) Repeat, repeat, repeat, repeat...

GOEBBELS: Make the stars revolve around the earth...

HESS: Tell a man his race is damned from birth...

GOEBBELS: Teach the public eye that Rome is Greece...

HESS: Pound the message home that war means peace...

ALL: (*singing*)

    Tell the Big Lie—
    It's the Truth,
    It's the Truth
      if it's told
        long enough...

GOEBBELS:

    Big Lies will bring you triumph sweet
    If you repeat, repeat, repeat...

ALL: (*echoing*) Repeat, repeat, repeat, repeat...

STREICHER: Sell cheap things in a fancy box...

GRAF: It won't smell like skunk if you call it fox...

ROEHM: Repetition is the road to wealth...

HESS: If it makes you sick, pretend it's health!...

ALL: (*singing*)

    Tell the Big Lie—
    It's the Truth,
    It's the Truth
      if it's told
        long enough...

GOEBBELS: Big Lies will bring you triumph sweet
If you repeat, repeat, repeat...

ALL: (*echoing*) Repeat, repeat, repeat, repeat...

GOERING AND GRAF: Hire muscle-men to protect the State...

HESS AND HIMMLER: Teach the small to venerate the Great...

ROEHM AND STREICHER:
Big Lies will bring you triumph sweet...

ALL: If you repeat, repeat, repeat!

Tell the Big Lie—
It's the Truth,
It's the Truth
  if it's told
    long enough...

GOEBBELS:
(*whispering at the head of the line as they exit in an eerie, grotesque version of a vaudeville line*)
Big Lies will bring you triumph sweet—
If you repeat, repeat, repeat...

ALL: (*as they go out—very softly*)
Repeat, repeat, repeat, repeat...

Scene 3—Old Shatterhand to Power

(*Impatiently* KARL MAY *steps forward to address* HITLER.)

KARL MAY: Repeat, repeat, that's all you still do. I won't permit you to be alone in history...(*pointing indignantly at the swastika flag*) You never got your swastika right. The Indian swastika runs the other way to keep the luck in. Your swastika is turned around the wrong way with the luck running out!

HITLER: (*soothingly, turning on his charm as if back in a dream childhood.*)

Come here, old man...(*Aside*) These dreamers must learn about dreams. (*He puts his arm around* MAY *and sits down with him*) You know when I was a boy the first thing I read of your kind of western story was *The Last of the Mohicans*... But a friend told me, "Fenimore Cooper is nothing. You must read Karl May."

MAY: That's right. Fenimore Cooper is nothing. I, Karl May, am the most popular writer in the world of western stories.

HITLER: Yes, I devoured all of your books, Karl May. I fell in love with your hero, Old Shatterhand...

MAY: (*dreamily*) Old Shatterhand...

HITLER: He used to cry "I am great! I am marvelous!" after each victory.

MAY: (*grudgingly*) But you should have gotten the swastika right.

HITLER: Never mind about the swastika. In Germany we need room to live in...You were my geographer...You showed me how to create a new west, new frontiers of our own with their raw, heroic virtues...

MAY: The west was open, free...That's what I tried to show in my books, the space, the freedom...

HITLER: Freedom, yes, for the strong...Freedom is always for the strong.

MAY: (*sharply*) Old Shatterhand knew what to do...

HITLER: (*dreaming*)

Old Shatterhand...He isn't afraid to act. He kills the thieving Indians. He shows how the strongest race conquers.

MAY: The strongest race, yes. But don't forget my great Apache leader, Winnetou.

HITLER: (*laughing*)

> How can I forget Winnetou? I love him... Why not? Everyone in Germany had his favorite Jew, just like your West where everyone had his favorite Indian. But the Indians had to die like the Jews...

MAY: (*indignantly*) Winnetou will never die!

HITLER:

> Old Shatterhand is destiny. He has to triumph. (*smiling*) You know I'm Old Shatterhand...

MAY: (*haughtily*)

> Never. You can't even turn the swastika the right way.

HITLER: (*laughing, patting May's shoulder*)

> Forget the swastika. You still don't understand. You were dead when I defeated senile old Hindenburg, when I became Chancellor...

MAY: (*drawing away*) You're not Old Shatterhand...

HITLER: (*smiling*)

> I became Old Shatterhand... Don't you see? Hindenburg was like a senile western sheriff who permits the outlaw Indians to flourish...

MAY: (*indignantly*)

> No, Hindenburg was Germany's greatest war hero. Millions of Germans donated one mark to the Red Cross. They won the right to pound a nail into the giant, wooden statue of Hindenburg that stood in Berlin outside of the Reichstag building. I'll show you...
>
> > (MAY *transforms himself into the tall figure of* HINDENBURG *hunched in aged, sombre senility. An actor steps forward to play* HINDENBURG'S *son, a Colonel in army uniform who wipes his father's forehead, listens to his mutterings, dusts the hunting trophies and the picture of the Virgin Mary above* HINDENBURG.)

HITLER: (*gleefully*)

> Hindenburg was only our hitching post. As we Nazis rode through the city we hitched our horses to him.

MAY: (*transforming himself as* HINDENBURG)

> He was our great Field Marshall. Six feet five inches tall, more than two hundred pounds. How his blue eyes glittered above his flowing mustache that cut the air like a sabre...

HITLER:

> He lived on too long. When I rode in to meet him he lived in a tomb of war relics, battle flags, hunting trophies, and an enormous collection of pictures of the Virgin Mary. His son, a Colonel, had to wipe his nose. When the Army begged Hindenburg to run for President he was already a muttering seventy-seven years old...

HINDENBURG-MAY: (*muttering to his son*)

> I want my peace...I want my peace...(MAY *emphasizes*) *Peace*, that's what he wanted...

HITLER: (*mimicking* HINDENBURG)

> *I want my peace*...How can such an idiot keep order in the wilderness that Germany has become? We need Old Shatterhand to keep order. With the help of our bully-boys I made Goering Chairman of the Parliament, the Reichstag...(*calling*) Hermann, come here!

GOERING: (*entering, cautiously*)

> You forgive me, Fuehrer?

HITLER: (*with a gracious gesture*)

> For the moment. Climb into your seat, Hermann. Show how it went in our frontier days...
>
> (*Gleefully,* GOERING *climbs into the Chairman's seat and bangs his gavel.* HINDENBURG-MAY *stares, dazed, as if caught in a nightmare.*)

GOERING: Order! Order in the Reichstag! Order!

HITLER: (*with a malicious smile as* HINDENBURG-MAY *totters down on his son's arm and prepares painfully to read his acceptance speech*)

> When Hindenburg was elected President he had to read his acceptance speech from a paper on which the letters were printed so large you could read them from the visitor's gallery through a pair of opera glasses.

(*Satirically* HITLER *looks through a pair of opera glasses at the scene.* HINDENBURG-MAY *reads his acceptance speech painfully and laboriously from an enormous sheet of paper that his son hands him.*)

HINDENBURG-MAY: (*we hear only a mumble and a few distinct words*)

...the German Republic...*Republic*...maintain constitutional integrity...*Vigilance*...Vigilance of the *law*...

HITLER: (*sneering*)

Vigilance of the law...You never knew what that meant. Old Shatterhand was waiting with his troopers ready. Then we were betrayed. Our own S.A. men turned into renegade Indians...

(ROEHM *stalks on stage as if fighting again his confinement in a historical dream. He is wearing an Indian headdress and a painted face over his S.A. uniform.*)

HINDENBURG-MAY: Who is that?

HITLER: One of your traitorous redskins, Ernst Roehm. Old Shatterhand must punish him...

ROEHM: (*doggedly*)

Some mistake has occurred. I Ernst Roehm was never an Indian...I don't accept my fate...From my childhood I had only one thought, one wish—to be a soldier...

GOERING: (*banging on his gavel*)

Out of order! The Fuehrer banishes you. You're an outlaw...

HITLER: (*screaming*) Roehm, you redskin traitor...

ROEHM: (*doggedly*)

There has been some mistake...(*feeling the paint on his face*) My face...

HITLER: (*accusing* ROEHM)

With your insane militaristic dream you tried to take over the army and state...

ROEHM: (*addressing* HINDENBURG-MAY)

As leader of our Nazi street army, the S.A., I demand, President Hindenburg, that our defense organization be represented in the Reichstag.

GOERING: (*banging his gavel*)
>Impossible. We don't accept Jewish Indians in the Reichstag.

HINDENBURG-MAY: (*to his son*)
>We must save the country from these gunmen.

ROEHM: (*blindly, doggedly*)
>The National Socialist movement is a fighting movement of the people, not the aristocrats...

GOERING: (*banging his gavel and roaring*)
>Silence! We'll fix you if you don't shut up...

HITLER: (*screaming*)
>Indian renegade...Treason...You traitor...

HINDENBURG-MAY: (*muttering to his son*)
>We must stop these outlaws...Restore frontier justice... That Austrian corporal, Hitler...He thinks he's Old Shatterhand...He's only a corporal, a lowly corporal...We must have the King back...The Kaiser...

HINDENBURG'S SON: (*wiping his father's face*)
>Yes, father. Don't agitate yourself. The army will take care of these redskins.

HITLER: (*shrieking*)
>Treason...Get rid of Roehm...He betrayed us to the redskins...

ROEHM: It's not true...Why can't I get rid of this paint?...If Adolf wants to kill me he'll have to do it himself...We call each other by our first names...I'm Ernst...He's Adolf...

HITLER: No one calls me Adolf anymore. I'm the Fuehrer. I'm Old Shatterhand.

GOERING: (*banging his gavel gleefully*)
>My Orders! I give our SS troops full legal powers to curb the S.A.

HITLER: Shut up. In Bavaria I assumed personal charge of supressing the revolt...

>(As Old Shatterhand he accepts a western Stetson hat from the ARCHITECT)

A disgusting scene of savage vice, redskin bestiality...

>(With the ARCHITECT and several other actors he pretends to ride a posse of horses against the S.A.)

From the Munich airport we sped to the hotel on the Tegernsee where Roehm and his SA savages were sleeping after their debauchery...

>(They rein in the horses as they dismount in front of the hotel.)

SS GUARD: (*after storming into the hotel he stops short, peering*)

>Fuehrer, look! It's Edmund Heines, the SA Obergruppenfuehrer of Silesia. He's in bed with a boy.

HITLER: Shoot him! (*Turning*) Where's that traitor, Roehm?

>(SS GUARD *brings* ROEHM *forward*)

HITLER: Strip him...(The SS GUARD *strips* ROEHM *to the waist*)

ROEHM: (*protesting*)

>Adolf, I fought with you in the streets. We're old comrades...

HITLER: (*ranting at him*)

>I'm your Fuehrer. After all these years how can you betray me?...All you want is military power. You think you can become Chief of Staff...

ROEHM: (*still in his stubborn trance of time*)

>From my childhood I've had only one thought—to be a soldier...

HITLER: Germany is more than an army...Germany is racial destiny...

ROEHM: The S.A. remains Germany's destiny

HITLER: (*enraged*)

>How many times do you and your degenerate redskins have to learn the price of treachery? (*to the SS man*) Give him a pistol.

>(*The SS man puts a pistol beside* ROEHM)

ROEHM: (*looking slowly at the pistol*) What's this?

>(*As the SS man turns away* ROEHM *tosses him the gun and says scornfully*)

>If you want to kill me do it yourself, *Adolf*...

HITLER CONT'D

HITLER: (*furiously*) Shoot the redskin swine.

HINDENBURG-MAY: (*suddenly jolted into speaking*)
> No, shoot him yourself, Old Shatterhand.

HITLER: (*ignoring* HINDENBURG-MAY) Kill him.
> (As ROEHM *stands at military attention the SS guard shoots him down.*)

GOERING: (*pounding his gavel with glee*)
> All over Berlin we killed the corrupt redskins.

HITLER: (*crying out eerily and waving his Stetson*)
> I am great...I am marvelous...

HINDENBURG-MAY: (*recoiling*)
> Old Shatterhand's cry...(*protesting*) No, you're not Old Shatterhand...

HITLER: (*crying again, mockingly*)
> I am great...I am marvelous...

HINDENBURG-MAY: (*muttering and shaking*)
> That Austrian Corporal...Shooting everybody like a wild west show...

HITLER: (*shouting*)
> You'll never forgive me, Hindenburg, because I was only a corporal. You insulted Old Shatterhand. At our first meeting you received me standing up. You wouldn't let Old Shatterhand sit down. You, the President of a collapsing redskin-infested government, tried to humilate me by forcing me to stand...

> (HINDENBURG-MAY *rises to icily to portray the meeting.*)

HINDENBURG-MAY:
> Herr Hitler, because of the dangerous situation I cannot transfer the power of government to your new, untried party. Your National Socialist Party does not even command a majority. It is intolerant of other groups, noisy, undisciplined...(*getting more and more agitated*) Your stormtroopers have clashed with the police...You have committed excessive violence against the Jews...All of these incidents have convinced me that certain unruly elements in your Party are beyond your control.

HITLER: *(aside to* GOERING) Will the old fool never stop talking?

HINDENBURG-MAY: (*with increasing agitation*)

> You must give up your one-sided idea of complete power... Cooperate with the parties of the Right and Center...Only then can you eliminate the widespread fear that a National Socialist government will misuse its power. However, if you can secure a workable majority in the Reichstag for a *positive* program—mind you I say a *definite, positive* program...

HITLER: Old Shatterhand has such a positive program in mind...

HINDENBURG-MAY: (*persisting*)

> If you can present this workable majority and the positive program, I will give you the chancellorship.

HITLER: (*immediately*) I accept.

HINDENBURG-MAY: (*quavering on*)

> Otherwise I offer you the Vice-Chancellorship under Von Papen. Von Papen will rule as President by emergency decree...

HITLER: (*in a furious outburst*)

> Von Papen! That unknown rabbit! Only I am great...Shoot them all!
>
> (*Sounds of street fighting, shouts of* "Down with the Republic," "Hitler for Chancellor," "Old Shatterhand to the Rescue," *etc.*)
>
> I am great...I am marvelous...

GOERING: (*banging his gavel triumphantly as shots and machine gun bursts are heard*)

> Burn the Reichstag! Old Shatterhand knows how to burn redskin villages...Burn the Reichstag...Blame the fire on the redskins...Burn the Reichstag.
>
> (*A glow of fire is seen.*)

HITLER: (*stepping up to* HINDENBURG-MAY *with a decree*)

> In view of the savage disorders created by the burning of the Reichstag, you must sign this emergency decree.
>
> (*He presents the decree.*)

HINDENBURG-MAY: (*glaring at him*) Emergency decree?

HITLER: To protect the People and the State against Communistic violence. Sign this defensive measure.

(*He holds the decree close to* HINDENBURG-MAY'S *weak eyes.*)

HINDENBURG-MAY: (*reading with mumbling comprehension as the cast erupts into an Indian Ragtime choral reaction:* The Chorale of Censorship:)

Restrictions on...personal...lib—er—ty...

CAST: (*singing to* HITLER)

I am great...I am marvelous...
Re—strict—shuns...on per—son—al...lib—er—ty...

HINDENBURG-MAY: (*speaking, mumbling*)

Restrictions...on the rights of assembly...and association...

CAST: (*singing*)

I am great...I am marvelous...
Re—strict—shuns...on the rights...of as—sem—bly...
and of...as—so—ci—a—*shun*...

HINDENBURG-MAY: (*mumbling*)

Violations...of the privacy...of postal, telegraphic...
and telephonic communications...

CAST: (*singing*)

I am great...I am marvelous...
Vio—la—*shuns*...of the privacy...
of pos—tal...tele—graph—sick...
tele—phoney...commun—ic—a—*shuns*...

HINDENBURG-MAY: (*mumbling*)

Warrants for house searches...Confiscations of property...
Emergency situation...

CAST: (*singing*)

I am great...I am marvelous...
War—rents...for house sear—ches...
Con—fis—ca—shuns...of pro—per—tyy...
E—mer—gen—cyyy...E—mer—gen—cyyyy...

37

HITLER: (*joining in exultantly, singing eerily*)

    Sign here without fear...
    E—mer—gen—cyy...E—mer—gen—cyyyy...
    I am marvelous to see
    In an e—mer—gen—cyy...

CAST: (*singing*)

    I am great...I am marvelous...

HINDENBURG-MAY: (*crying out at end of final chorus*)

    No, you're not Old Shatterhand!

HITLER: (*with new, brisk authority*)

    Farewell, Hindenburg. I sentence you to live forever in the pantheon of German history. Play the role of noble Winnetou, the honorable Apache warrior who sacrifices himself for his lost people.

    (*Mockingly* GOERING *puts an Indian headdress on* HINDENBURG-MAY)

HINDENBURG-MAY: (*crying out*)

    No, Winnetou is *my* glorious warrior!

HITLER: (*as members of the cast begin to sing a jagged version of the Horst Wessel song*)

    Bury Hindenburg! Let the dying old Field Marshall serve as a warrior-symbol of our national power. Die with honor, noble Winnetou!

HINDENBURG-MAY: (*another agonized protest*)

    No, Winnetou lives forever!

HITLER: (*riding over the protest*)

    Today and forever here in the Cathedral of Ice a magnificent ceremony of solemn dedication is unveiled to the German people and to the world.

    (*an SS man has been helping* HITLER *to put on a long formal cutaway coat*)

    In this cathedral lie buried the sacred bones of Frederick the Great...Here the Hohenzollern kings are worshipped. Here I convene the Reichstag to inaugurate my new Empire...

(*As if hypnotized in time by the transformation of the old church at Potsdam into the Cathedral of Ice,* HINDENBURG-MAY *begins to totter down the aisle in his Indian headdress. The actors cheer him on mockingly.*)

HITLER: Now President Hindenburg pauses before the empty seat of honor reserved in the imperial gallery in memory of Kaiser Wilhelm the Second.

(*The empty seat of honor lights up in an intense white glare. In a daze* HINDENBURG *salutes the ghost of Kaiser Wilhelm.*)

Heil Winnetou! Heil Kaiser Wilhelm!

CAST: Heil Hitler!...Heil Hitler!...Heil Hitler!

(*Mockingly* HITLER *raises his hand to acknowledge the applause as he becomes chancellor again in memory. Slowly several SS men emerge to central positions as* HITLER *begins to speak in acceptance of the chancellorship. The rhythm of the play changes abruptly from the mockery of the ghost-like historical ceremony at Potsdam to the sense of cold, impersonal, secret police power.*)

HITLER: (*bowing to* HINDENBURG-MAY)

Thanks to you, Herr Generalfeldmarschall, we celebrate in this historic place the union between our ancient Prussian greatness and our new international strength. We pay you homage, Winnetou. Here in this immortal cathedral of power Providence reveals itself. A divine spirit protects the new forces of our great destiny.

(*With a "show of deep humility," as Shirer describes it,* HITLER *bows low to* HINDENBURG-MAY *and grips the aged President's hand firmly. Slowly* HITLER'S *hand-shake turns into a macabre death-grip. The SS troopers move together singing the Horst Wessel song: "Raise high the flags! Stand rank on rank together. Storm troopers march with steady, quiet tread, etc."*)

HINDENBURG-MAY: (*crying out*)

Wait...*Please*...Bury Winnetou with honor...

HITLER: (*releasing his grip on the dead* HINDENBURG-MAY, *signalling as the troopers stop singing abruptly and stand frozen in time*)

HITLER CONT'D
> Old Shatterhand has conquered.
>> (*Suddenly he lets out his uncontrollable whoop of triumph, throwing away his western hat*)
>
> I am great!...I am marvelous!
>> (*Then with proper historical humility again he orders:*)
>
> Bury him with honor. Bury Winnetou's ghost.
>> (*Hand over his heart, he stands at attention as banners of black crepe fall down and* HIMMLER *moves his SS men around coldly, gesturing with his riding crop.*)

KARL MAY: (*jolted out of his* HINDENBURG *death-trance, accusing* HITLER)
> No, Winnetou is not dead. You're *not* Old Shatterhand. My west is not like this. My west is open, adventurous, free...

HITLER: (*ignoring him, extending his arm*)
> Heil Hitler! We're in power forever. Sing! (*The Horst Wessel song starts again*) Vanish in history, Winnetou. Heil Old Shatterhand!

CAST: (*echoing*) Heil Old Shatterhand!...Heil Hitler!

HINDENBURG-MAY: (*as he collapses, shouting desperately*)
> You're not Old Shatterhand...You're not my hero...Old Shatterhand is a legend, an immortal myth!
>> (*As* HITLER *stands at attention, his arm extended, ignoring* HINDENBURG-MAY'S *dying protests,* HIMMLER *supervises the SS men. They lift up* HINDENBURG-MAY'S *body as if carrying it in a funeral procession. Singing the Horst Wessel song they carry out* HINDENBURG-MAY'S *body.*)

Scene 4—Wagner And Hitler At Bayreuth

(*Abruptly the Horst Wessel song dissolves into a rapt chorus singing the "Awake" chorus from* WAGNER'S Die Meistersinger. *Cheers as the* FUEHRER *and the* ARCHITECT *enter the Dictator's box at the Bayreuth Festspielhaus.* HITLER *waves and graciously acknowledges the applause. He points out the details of the auditorium to the* ARCHITECT *as if to show his affinity with Bayreuth.*)

ARCHITECT: (*extremely impressed*)
> Marvelous, Fuehrer. What a privilege to visit Bayreuth with you again, to hear *Tristan and Isolde*.

HITLER: (*with anticipation*) Wait till you see who's conducting.

ARCHITECT: Have you summoned back Furtwaengler?

HITLER: That Jew-lover? An impossible snob...

ARCHITECT: (*his attention riveted suddenly on the conductor who enters*)
> Look!... It can't be...

HITLER: (*with childish delight*) Of course it is.

ARCHITECT: (*entranced by the romance of it all*)
> Fuehrer, I don't believe it... It's *Wagner*.

HITLER: If King Ludwig could have his private performance of Wagner why can't I?

ARCHITECT: (*hastily*) Who can deny you?

WAGNER: (*rapping with his baton for attention*)
> Please pay attention, Fuehrer. The key to an understanding of destiny is *Liebestod*.

HITLER: The Love-Death... I'm ready, Herr Wagner.

WAGNER: Fame, honor... Nothing of that kind can refresh me. My only need is love.

HITLER: (*nostalgically*) We all need to make people love us.

WAGNER: (*sharply*)
> You fail to understand that true love requires sacrifice— *Liebestod*.

HITLER: I understand, Maestro, love as death. (*to the* ARCHITECT) Wagner likes to lecture me.

WAGNER: (*waving his baton*)
> Tristan and Isolde, the greatest love ever portrayed...
>> (*He begins to conduct the Love-Death sequence from* Tristan and Isolde. *Two actors appear miming the roles as the music is heard on tape.*)

HITLER: (*sinking moodily into the music*)

>Yours is the greatest German music ever written, Herr Wagner.

WAGNER: (*as he conducts and speaks, the music is heard softly in the background*)

>Do you hear the bliss of quitting life? Can you feel the glory of dying to find redemption? Entering that world of wonder is forbidden if we try to enter by force. Dare we call it *Death?* Or is it the wonderful world of night? The night when an ivy and a vine spring up in locked embrace over Tristan and Isolde's marriage-grave...

HITLER: (*brooding*) Marriage-grave...The wonderful world of night...

WAGNER: (*conducting with an exuberant burst*)

>Night is the time for love. The time when love frees us from nightmares and becomes our salvation. (*conducting sensuously*) Listen to the ecstasy of Tristan embracing Isolde. For the first time I portray the climax of physical love in music...

HITLER: Superb. How fascinating. (*to the* ARCHITECT) The singers are fully clothed too. That permits the imagination to work.

WAGNER: (*conducting vigorously*)

>Love's dreams endure beyond mere sexual acts...Love triumphs over every obstacle...

ISOLDE: (*stopping the music abruptly, she turns, speaks to* WAGNER)

>Maestro! Maestro! I can't hear myself. Can you please have the orchestra play a little softer?

WAGNER: (*bristling*)

>Impossible. Here the orchestra carries the passion. You must sing louder, clearer...Try just speaking the words for Herr Hitler...

>(WAGNER *resumes conducting as the music starts again.*)

ISOLDE: (*reciting passionately*)

>"...To drown in the infinity
>Of the World Spirit,
>To sink into
>The Void of Thought
>Is the highest bliss!"

WAGNER: (*transformed as* ISOLDE *dies over* TRISTAN'S *body*)

>The Void of Thought...There's poetry for you. They die and live forever. Ressurection—the immortality of love...

HITLER: (*transfigured, meditating*)

>If only the whole world could die this way. (*to* WAGNER) Maestro, what a privilege it would be to die your heroic Love-Death.

WAGNER: (*haughtily*) The world can be transformed only by art.

HITLER: Or by politics.

WAGNER: (*contradicting him*)

>No, the politician rules briefly. The great artist endures until the end of time.

HITLER: (*to the* ARCHITECT)

>You see what I mean by ego? This Bayreuth theatre of Wagner's is nothing compared to what we'll build.

WAGNER: (*suspiciously*) Did you criticize my theatre?

HITLER: (*hastily*)

>No, Maestro. Please continue. (*petulantly to the* ARCHITECT) Wagner has no appreciation of my ability as an architect.

WAGNER: (*turning, calling to* TRISTAN AND ISOLDE *who are still lying immortally dead on stage*)

>Rise now. We'll return to the Love-Death.

TRISTAN: (*staggering up in dazed humility*)

>Maestro, every time I sing your immortal work I find it more difficult to return to this mundane world.

WAGNER: (*snapping*)

>Of course. You're finally learning the work.

HITLER: (*to the* ARCHITECT, *echoing* WAGNER'S *criticism of the tenor*)

>Mundane world. What does that tenor know of the world?

TRISTAN: (*protesting to* WAGNER) Maestro, it's a long, difficult part.

WAGNER: Do you think love and death are short, simple?

TRISTAN: (*abjectly*) No, Maestro, I didn't mean...

WAGNER: (*furiously*)

> You still don't understand the depth of character in Tristan. Only the future will understand Tristan.

HITLER: (*leaning forward intently*)

> That's right, Maestro. I will show the world the meaning of *Tristan*.

WAGNER: (*rapping with his baton for attention*)

> Again, the Liebestod...(*warning* TRISTAN) Remember, Tristan, you must really wish to die for love.

HITLER: (*to the* ARCHITECT)

> Now we'll hear something great.
>
> > (*The music from the famous Act II, Scene 2 sequence is heard on tape.* WAGNER *conducts triumphantly with increasing passion. As the voices soar out* HITLER *translates rapturously, as if transformed by the meaning of the words.*)

HITLER: (*speaking the lines that the singers are singing on tape*)

> > "Eternal night,
> > Sweetest night...
> > Loftiest night of Love!
> > Those whom you seize,
> > Those whom you trance,
> > How can they ever wish
> > To wake from your sleep?
> > Fear is now banished...
> > Gracious Death,
> > We yearn for your mercy,
> > Your Love-In-Death..."
>
> > (*transported, poking the* ARCHITECT, HITLER *shouts at* WAGNER)
>
> Give them no mercy, Death!

WAGNER: (*ecstatically as he conducts*)

> Death, you must die! Tristan and Isolde's love is too strong for you...

HITLER: (*as* TRISTAN AND ISOLDE *continue their duet*)

"Within your arms
We find your peace, Death...
Your ancient, holy warmth
Freed from Life's awakening..."

The peace of Death...

WAGNER: (*conducting radiantly*)

Redemption! Freedom from death. My Love-Death!

(*The cast picks this up mockingly around the theatre in a sound-poem based on the syllables* Love-Death. *This sound-poem and the music with* WAGNER *conducting fervently continue under* HITLER'S *final speech to the end of the scene.*)

Sound Poem On *Love-Death*

Looooh...
Loooov—aaalll...
Loooov—debt...
Loooov—*debt*...
Loooov—deaaarth...
Loooov—deaaaaarth...
Loooov—Eaaaarth...
Loooooov—Breaaaaath...
Loooooov—Breaaaaaaaath...
Loooooov—Deaaaaaaaath...
Love-Death...
Love-*Death*...
Love-Death!...

HITLER: (*entranced, magnetized, he speaks so forcefully that the* ARCHITECT *shrinks back in fear*)

Our Love-Death! Eternally our Love-Death in the Cathedral of Ice. Maestro, you have found the cure for the world's problems. However weak a man may be, when he acts as Providence directs he becomes immeasurably strong. Anyone who interferes with his divine mission becomes an enemy of the people. Maestro, I give you my sacred word. As Fuehrer I will turn the world into the greatest Love-Death it has ever seen!

Scene 5—Sentimental Interlude

(*Creating an immediate strange, sentimental contrast to Tristan and Isolde, a banal 1930s musical comedy "Love-Death" song is heard, "The Ballad of German Love." It is sung by two nervous, popular young film stars whom* EVA BRAUN *and* HITLER *have invited to their sanctuary. The scene is another reflection of* HITLER'S *desire to re-create his dream memories of Berchtesgaden.* HITLER *is going over some of his favorite architectural projects with the* ARCHITECT. GOERING *and* GOEBBELS, *forced to be present for another long evening, already show their impatience to escape. During this scene until page 67* HITLER *does not wear the Jewish coat.*)

TWO SINGERS: (*singing "The Ballad of German Love."*)

MAN	Love is a tree of many leaves
WOMAN	Love is the sentiment that always grieves...
TOGETHER	Love is a spiderweb of doubt, Love is a mystery within, without!
MAN	Who will find love must look within...
WOMAN	Our German love is immortal sin...
TOGETHER	Who will find love must look without For love must always smile, never doubt.
	Love is a tree of many leaves, Love is the sentiment that always grieves. Our German love will conquer the sun When we two become eternally one!

EVA BRAUN: (*entranced*)

    Aren't they marvelous singers, Adolf? Let's watch their new film. I can hardly wait...

HITLER: (*waving her off*)

    In a moment, Eva. I'm discussing a proper memorial with my architect.

EVA: (*dejected*) Yes, Adolf.

GOERING: (*fidgeting uneasily, determined to steal away*)

    If you don't mind, Fuehrer, please excuse me. I have an important appointment. (*He gets up to leave.*)

HITLER: (*aside, maliciously*)

> He's off to steal another picture or lounge around in one of his fancy costumes.

GOERING: (*aside*)

> I can't stand another boring evening. (*to* HITLER) Good night, Fuehrer. I hope you enjoy your film. (*He exits.*)

GOEBBELS: (*hesitantly*)

> Fuehrer, I too must leave. I'm sure you'll enjoy their new musical film, *Love In The Alps*.

HITLER: (*suspiciously*) Is it about skiing? I hate skiing.

GOEBBELS: There's hardly any skiing. It's based on a Lehar operetta.

HITLER: Good, I love operettas.

GOEBBELS: Please excuse me, Fuehrer. (*He goes.*)

HITLER: (*maliciously*)

> Goebbels is off to climb into bed with another of his film girls. If I were his wife...(*calling*) Bormann!

BORMANN: (*appearing*) Yes, Fuehrer.

HITLER: Let's have the film.

BORMANN: (*aside to the fidgeting singers*) Don't be so nervous.

> (*He pinches the woman singer.*)

HITLER: (*aside to the* ARCHITECT))

> Who wouldn't be nervous with Bormann around? He puts his nose into everything...This place is beginning to look like the cheap interior decorations on an ocean liner.

ARCHITECT: (*unrolling plans*) I think you'll find these plans exciting.

HITLER: (*to the singers*)

> I've heard a great deal about your popularity with young people.

YOUNG MALE SINGER: (*stiff with fear he salutes*)

> Fuehrer, it is a privilege to be here.

EVA: (*excitedly*)

> Oh, Adolf, I heard them in Munich in *Fledermaus*. They were so good...(*to the singers*) Your new song is all the rage.

HITLER: (*to the* ARCHITECT)

    Yes, their song was quite good, don't you think?

ARCHITECT: (*a little grimly*) Excellent.

HITLER: (*to* EVA *and the singers*) We'll be with you in a moment.

YOUNG MALE SINGER: Certainly Fuehrer.

YOUNG FEMALE SINGER: We are overjoyed to be here.

    (*As the singers converse nervously with* EVA, HITLER *talks to the* ARCHITECT *about the plans.*)

ARCHITECT: (*pointing at the plans*)

    There's one difficulty here. To achieve the right space, we must move the Nuernberg Zoo.

HITLER: Why not? We'll give them a new, more beautiful zoo. (*pointing*) This is the marching area for our troops?

ARCHITECT: Yes.

HITLER: Is that large enough?

ARCHITECT:

    Larger than the palace areas of Kings Darius and Xerxes at the height of their power in fifth century Persepolis...

HITLER: (*pointing*) What about the stands here?

ARCHITECT:

    Seats for 160,000 spectators. And this central viewing platform for important guests is crowned by a large sculpture of a woman.

HITLER: Is it larger than the Statue of Liberty?

ARCHITECT: Ours will be forty-six feet higher.

HITLER: Excellent. Everything must be simple, in good taste.

ARCHITECT: The problem of the stadium is difficult.

HITLER: I want the stadium to hold 400,000 people.

ARCHITECT: (*hastily*)

    As you can see it's designed to be larger than the Circus Maximus in Rome which held almost 200,000 people. Our stadium will have a volume three times that of the Pyramid of Cheops...

HITLER: Good. You wonder why I want to build the biggest monuments in history?

ARCHITECT: I understand.

HITLER: Each German must have his self-respect restored. To every German I want to say—we are not inferior. We are equal to and superior to every other nation.

ARCHITECT:
It is a great cause. However, my staff has estimated the costs and...

HITLER: (*gesturing impatiently*)
Bormann will take care of the costs. That's the only reason I keep him around—to raise money.

ARCHITECT: (*pointing to some figures*)
The cost may be as much as a billion marks.

HITLER: (*waving this aside*)
That's less than two battleships of the *Bismarck* class. These monuments will stand forever. When the Finance Minister asks their cost don't answer him. Let him stew...Come, let's watch the film. I'm very pleased with your plans.

(*He crosses to congratulate the singers who relax visibly.* HITLER *converses with them, asking* "Would you like a cup of tea or a glass of wine?" *etc.*)

EVA: (*talking to the* ARCHITECT)
Bormann is after that secretary again. That man is disgusting. I don't see how his wife stands him.

ARCHITECT: (*shrugging*) Perhaps because they have six children.

EVA: He's sickening. Whenever the Fuehrer is near Bormann moons over his wife and children as if they were his only treasure. He calls her sweetheart mine, dearest heart, even beloved mummy-girl.

ARCHITECT: Beloved mummy-girl?

EVA: (*indignantly*)
Can you believe it? Then he runs off to chase another secretary.

ARCHITECT: (*as* HITLER *returns*) Shh...

HITLER: We're ready. Start the film, please.

> (HITLER *and* EVA *sit in adjacent chairs. Deliberately the* ARCHITECT *sits as far behind them as possible, since he too is bored with these occasions but can't escape. The film is shown flickering offstage, invisible to the audience.* HITLER *and* EVA *begin to gossip.*)

EVA: You'll like this actress. She's very entertaining.

HITLER: She has excellent posture.

EVA: They sing so well together.

HITLER: She has attractive legs too.

EVA: (*pouting*) Don't you like my legs?

HITLER: You're wearing high heels again. You know I don't like high heels.

EVA: (*defiantly*) They're quite flat.

HITLER: (*pointing to her shoes*)

> Look at them. It's bad for your health to wear such high heels.

EVA: (*gesturing at the film*)

> You don't mind that actress wearing high heels.

HITLER: (*protesting*)

> It's only a musical comedy. You must look after yourself.

EVA: (*pouting, concentrating on the film*)

> She's really excellent in *her high heels*. She reminds me a little of Jenny Jugo.

HITLER: Not at all. She's more like Henny Porten. Her smile.

EVA: She seems so happy.

HITLER: That's what a film should be.

EVA: Why can't we have more entertaining films like this?

HITLER: Goebbels doesn't value entertainment enough. That's what comes from being an intellectual. We must have films that appeal to the masses. Any true leader knows the masses are essentially feminine.

EVA: Feminine?

HITLER: (*smiling*) You don't convince audiences. You conquer them.

EVA: Even in a musical?

HITLER: In any kind of performance.

EVA: (*coquettishly*) What if I tried to conquer you?

HITLER: Women captivate, they don't conquer.

EVA: (*smiling*)
> Some day I'll test your theory. (*pointing at his tie*) You know, Adolf, you're wearing your old tie again.

HITLER: I can't walk down the street blazing like a furnace.

EVA: Your ties are too drab. Every time I give you a bright new tie you go back to the old ones.

HITLER: You know how I feel about loud colors.

EVA: (*teasingly*)
> I'm going to test you. (*She rises.*) I'll be right back.

HITLER: Where are you going?

EVA: You'll see. (*She laughs and rushes out.*)

HITLER: (*calling after her*) What are you up to now, Eva?
> (*turning to the* ARCHITECT)
> Women—you never know what she'll do next.

ARCHITECT: (*rousing himself hastily, as he's been falling asleep like other members of* HITLER'S *entourage*)
> She's charming, Fuehrer.

HITLER: It's good to relax. All day long I hear nothing but heavy, noisy, masculine voices.

ARCHITECT: (*a little taken aback*) You're lucky to have Fraulein Braun.

HITLER:
> An attractive young thing—and she's loyal. Of course I had her investigated. Bormann took care of that. I couldn't have a mistress tainted with Jewish blood.

ARCHITECT: She's so fine looking.

HITLER: You can never tell where it's hiding. Did you know her sister worked for a Jewish doctor?

ARCHITECT: Really?

HITLER: I put a stop to that. (*complaining*) The problem always is Eva wants to marry me. What would I do with a wife?

ARCHITECT: It would be a burden, Fuehrer.

HITLER: Impossible for a man in my position. Heads of state should never marry. For you it's different... You can have a private life.

ARCHITECT: (*through the vision of his un-private life*) Yes, Fuehrer.

HITLER: You have your privacy, your family security, your wife and children.

ARCHITECT: (*unable to resist*) When I'm able to see them, Fuehrer.

HITLER: Why don't you invite your wife here? Come and live with me. I'll build you a house. (*then, reflecting*) You know the real reason why I can never marry?

ARCHITECT: Why, Fuehrer?

HITLER: Think of the danger if I had children.

ARCHITECT: I don't understand.

HITLER: Great men always have sick children. Napoleon's son... Goethe's son who was a cretin. How could I ever take such a risk?

ARCHITECT: I'm sure Fraulein Braun would never... She's so healthy.

HITLER: (*moodily*) I could never take the risk.

> (*Suddenly the film stops.* EVA BRAUN *has had it stopped. She enters in blackface as Al Jolson singing "Sonny Boy."* HITLER *is stunned. The* ARCHITECT *is frightened, afraid that* EVA'S *masquerade will bring on one of* HITLER'S *tantrums. The other watchers are tense, waiting to see what will happen.*)

EVA: (*after finishing her song and dance act she laughs and approaches* HITLER):

How do you like it, Adolf? I've been practising for you.

HITLER: (*slowly changing mood*) It's *you*, Eva.

> (EVA *does a final, gay turn around him.*)

HITLER: (*dissolving into laughter as everyone relaxes*)

    Eva, Eva, you funny girl... You are so funny...

EVA: I knew you'd like it.

HITLER: (*recovering himself*)

    You are naughty. This American, Al Jolson, is a Jewish entertainer.

EVA: (*laughing and patting him*) It's only a game. No one will ever tell.

HITLER: (*looking around at the subdued audience*) That is true. (*then laughing again as he pats* EVA) You are a little performer, Eva. Perhaps I should let you go on stage instead of keeping you to myself.

EVA: (*sparking*)

    I'm quite happy, Adolf, as long as you let me perform for you. (*then pouting*) But you keep me away so much. Can't we at least live together all the time?

HITLER: We'll see. If I can arrange it without any gossip.

EVA: (*with delight*) Oh, you promised. You promised.

HITLER: Come, let's go upstairs. If you don't take off that blackface you'll be stuck with it.

EVA: (*laughing*) That's an old witch's tale.

HITLER: Women are witches.

    (*As they approach the staircase the ghostly figure of* GELI RAUBAL, HITLER'S *niece with whom he lived before she committed suicide, appears on the staircase.*)

HITLER: I'm getting chilly. That damnable wind...(*He puts his hand up against the wind*)

EVA: Is something wrong? There's no south wind here.

HITLER: (*agitated*)

    It's blowing right through that window. Can't you feel how depressed it makes me? (*staring at* GELI) She hated that wind even more than I.

EVA: (*puzzled*) She?

HITLER: (*staring*)
> Don't you see her there? Geli... My niece, my love, Geli Raubal...

EVA: Don't keep tormenting yourself. Geli is dead. She killed herself.

GELI: (*mockingly to* HITLER) I died for you. I shot myself with *your* pistol.

HITLER: (*with immediate self-pity*)
> Yes, you died for me. I'll never forgive myself.

EVA: (*jealously*) You must forget her... She's dead.

HITLER: Why did she do it? (*to* GELI) I would have given you anything.

EVA: It wasn't your fault.

GELI: I want to go to Vienna to live my own life. I want to sing.

HITLER: (*angrily*)
> You want to make a whore of yourself. I couldn't let you leave me for that city of Jewish whores.

GELI: You keep me hidden away. You keep me a prisoner.

HITLER: (*hysterically*)I give you everything you want.

GELI: You won't marry me. You would never marry me.

HITLER: How can I? You're my niece... It would ruin me politically.

GELI: All you care about is politics.

HITLER: (*turning on* EVA *suddenly*)
> Get her away. She doesn't belong here. Why do you women keep threatening me with suicide?

EVA: That's not fair.

HITLER: (*hysterically*)
> You're all the same. Selfish witches if you don't get your way. (*to* EVA) Promise me you'll never try to commit suicide again.

EVA: (*confessing*) I was lonely. I didn't mean to kill myself.

HITLER: You were jealous of Geli, weren't you?

EVA: You stayed away from me for weeks at a time. When I found I was only wounded I called the doctor myself. I didn't want to die.

GELI: (*laughing*) I wanted to die, but I can't die...

HITLER: How can I trust you women? The nation demands my sacrifice. I give myself to it completely. Promise me you'll never do such a silly thing again.

EVA: I promise. You know how much I love you.

GELI: (*mockingly*) I promise. You know how much I love you.

HITLER: (*like a child to* EVA)

Forgive me, I need you. It's terrible how much I must demand of you...It takes great sacrifice to serve a man in my position...For the time being Germany must be my wife, do you understand?

EVA: (*soothingly*) I understand.

GELI: (*echoing* EVA *mockingly*) I understand.

HITLER: (*brightening*)

After my task is accomplished I promise you I'll retire with pleasure. I'll devote myself to artistic tasks. We'll live in these mountains, free from all the parasites that surround us. We'll be able to live together, travel wherever we wish. I'll have time to paint again, work on my architectural plans.

EVA: Don't worry, Adolf. I'll always do what you want. You know you can do anything you want with me.

GELI: (*echoing her mockingly*)

You know you can do anything you want with me. (*They draw him away as the scene ends.*)

Scene 6—The Fuehrer Rituals

(EVA *appears, wiping away her blackface. Moodily* HITLER *strides up on a platform, brooding on his private balcony, staring into the night and stars. High up we see one star twinkling.*)

EVA: As mistress of Hitler's home I practise invisibility. When the Fuehrer holds meetings or receives foreign diplomats I'm forced to disappear. A housekeeper takes care of everything. I made her my ally so Bormann couldn't operate behind my

EVA CONT'D

> back. A cook mixes all of the vegetarian foods that the Chief requires. (*smiling*) I like to call him the Chief! Whenever I can I smoke in secret. I fill the air with French perfume to cover the cigarette smell that the Chief hates. The Chief! (*she laughs, does a turn, and withdraws.*)

HITLER: (*brooding, looking at the stars*)

> The stars of heaven...What kind of worship is that? A Jew, Saul of Tarsus, created the Christian heaven...Look at the planets...Venus, Mars, Jupiter...They're not Christian...Man becomes great through struggle, not pity. States which offend this simple law fall into decay. Force is the first law. To transform the world the power of leadership must be recognized.
>
> (*The distant star twinkles, transformed into a swastika as if in* HITLER'S *mind. After a moment* HITLER *steps down from the balcony as an SS man enters followed by two genial Nazi Party officials, a man and a woman.*)

HITLER: Have you carried out my orders about the new greeting?

MALE PARTY OFFICIAL: (*reading instructions*)

> Yes, Fuehrer. The greeting of "Heil Hitler" will become the official greeting. It is no longer necessary to say "Hello" or "Gruss Gott" to a friend. To celebrate the Fuehrer say joyously, "Heil Hitler."

HITLER: Be sure to emphasize *joyously*. My government is supported by the entire people.

WOMAN PARTY OFFICIAL: (*continuing instructions*)

> If people are members of the same social group it is customary to raise the right arm at an angle so the palm of the hand becomes visible. (*she demonstrates*) As you raise your arm *joyously* say "Heil Hitler," or at least "Heil".

HITLER: Make sure to include "Hitler" after "Heil".

WOMAN PARTY OFFICIAL: (*correcting hastily*)

> The official greeting should include the complete, joyous name, "Heil Hitler."

MALE PARTY OFFICIAL: (*taking over from the distraught woman official*)

> If one sees an acquaintance in the distance (*He imitates seeing a distant acquaintance*) merely raise the right hand in the manner described. (*He demonstrates.*)

HITLER: (*annoyed*)

>Put it more positively. (*He demonstrates*) The pride of a people's greeting.

MALE PARTY OFFICIAL: (*He's nervous now too.*)

>If one encounters a person socially inferior, then stretch the right arm fully out at eye-level. (*he demonstrates*) At the same time say warmly with pride, "Heil Hitler!"

HITLER: That's better.

MALE PARTY OFFICIAL:

>(*encouraged he requests the woman official to take his right arm*)
>
>If your right arm is engaged by a lady as you walk down the street, the greeting should always be carried out with the left arm.
>
>(*He demonstrates with his left arm calling, "Heil Hitler!"*)

HITLER: (*nodding and smiling*)

>Always be courteous to women and children. The family is the germ-cell of the nation.
>
>(*A banner falls reading* THE FAMILY IS THE GERM-CELL OF THE NATION)

WOMAN PARTY OFFICIAL:

>Absolute priority, Fuehrer, must be given to a growing birthrate.

HITLER: (*reflecting*)

>Yes, the German mother is sacred. The problem is how to promote babies without having one myself. What if we award special medals to mothers? What if we give them the privilege of saying, "I have donated a child to the Fuehrer."
>
>(*The Party Officials indicate their enthusiasm. As if in a fantasy two mothers enter and line up before the Party Officials. They carry doll-babies to indicate their fertility. The* "Song of the Procreators and the Baby-Making Machines" *begins. It is interspersed through the next section:*)

Song Of The Procreators and The Baby-Making Machines

SS MEN: We are the Procreators...

WOMEN: We the Baby-Making Machines...

TOGETHER: Our duty is to mate,
For Germany create—
Four, five, or ten...

SS MEN: A Race of Supermen...

WOMEN: And Superwomen...

WOMAN PARTY OFFICIAL: (*proclaiming and giving medal*)

> The Party is proud to affirm that the German mother occupies the same honored place in the community as the front-line soldier...To Frau Inge Dorfmann, the Silver Honor Cross of the German Mother for bearing more than six children...

FRAU DORFMANN: (*as she accepts the medal*) Heil Hitler!

WOMAN PARTY OFFICIAL:

> To Frau Ortrud Grossobst, the Gold Honor Cross of the German Mother for bearing more than eight children...

HITLER: (*musing to himself*) Can you believe it? Eight children...

FRAU GROSSOBST: (*almost dropping some doll-babies—she has so many*)
> Heil Hitler!

MALE PARTY OFFICIAL:

> In the future all members of the Party's organizations will be duty-bound to salute wearers of the Mother's Honor Cross. Thus our citizens will pay homage to our German mothers.
>
> > (*There is a temporary crisis as they run out of candidates for German motherhood. The* WOMAN OFFICIAL *whispers frantically to* HITLER. *We hear her saying, "We do not have enough Mothers, etc."*)

HITLER: (*calling impatiently*)

> Himmler! Himmler! (HIMMLER *enters*) We are running out of sacred German mothers. Impossible. We must increase our population by stronger measures.

HIMMLER: Fuehrer, I'm pleased to report that our SS scientists have solved this problem. We have created the Lebensborn—the Spring of Life...

(*Another banner drops reading* LEBENSBORN—THE SPRING OF LIFE.)

HITLER: What is this Spring of Life?

HIMMLER: Our new SS Foundation for Unmarried Mothers. Their children are fathered by superior SS men and other racially valuable Germans.

HITLER: (*squirming a little*) We must be careful of illegitimacy. My father suffered from this curse.

HIMMLER: We will wipe out the disgrace of illegitimacy, Fuehrer. Every woman in our Lebensborn Foundation will consider it an honor to bear you a child.

(HIMMLER *steps forward to address the SS Lebensborn men.*)

Comrades, only he who leaves a child behind can die peacefully in battle. Beyond the bonds of bourgeois law German women, acting from a profound moral seriousness, have the sublime task of becoming mothers. You will be their temporary husbands. Destiny alone knows if you will return or die in battle for Germany. Your heritage of the strongest German stock must be passed on. (*pointing*) The red dot in our banner symbolizes the triumphant German embryos of future children. Heil Hitler!

(*As the* SS MEN *salute him in return,* HITLER *and* HIMMLER *exit.*)

SS MEN: (*singing*)   We are the Procreators...

TWO WOMEN CANDIDATES: (*singing as if on their way to the Lebensborn*)

    We the Baby-Making Machines...

TOGETHER: We'll make our country purer
By mating for our Fuehrer—
Four, five, or ten...

SS MEN: A Race of Supermen...

WOMEN CANDIDATES: And Superwomen...

WOMAN CANDIDATE I: Where are you going?

WOMAN CANDIDATE II:
> To the Lebensborn. I've been chosen to be impregnated for the Fuehrer.

WOMAN CANDIDATE I: So have I.

WOMAN CANDIDATE II: Isn't it a great honor?

> (*whispering and giggling anxiously they sit on a bench across from the* SS MEN.)

FIRST SS MAN: (*rubbing his arm*)
> They've taken enough blood out of us to service a regiment.

SECOND SS MAN: Sh, the doctor's coming.

SS DOCTOR: (*entering and addressing the* SS MEN)
> Your blood tests show that you belong to Group A—the pure Nordic group. After inquiries into your background, you've both been certified to come from pure Aryan stock. We've gone back as far as the 18th century to check your ancestors.

FIRST SS MAN: (*awed*) 18th century...

SS DOCTOR: (*continuing*)
> We German scientists have proved that generations preserve outstanding racial aptitudes. Bach, Beethoven, Wagner all belonged to a long line of superior musicians. The Krupp family has given Germany supreme inventors and military technicians. (*with a smile*) In your SS training I'm sure you've always admired thoroughbreds. Stud farms have proved that a fine mare mated with a purebred stallion will produce a champion thoroughbred—nine times out of ten.

> (*The* FIRST SS MAN *nudges his companion.*)

> Unfortunately modern science is still unable to cure all of the errors of heredity. In foreign countries an alcoholic may copulate with a Jew or a syphilitic. Within a few generations you have an abnormal population. Our race purification program is designed to produce that pure, regenerative blood which we need to carry out the Fuehrer's will.

FIRST SS MAN: We'll do our best, Sir.

(*The* SS DOCTOR *exits. Sentimental, romantic operetta music is heard. The* SS MEN *approach the women who are sitting, waiting.*)

FIRST WOMAN: (*to her companion*)

    I hope that dark one asks me. What's the matter with you?

SECOND WOMAN: I'm sorry... I feel a little as though I'm selling myself.

FIRST WOMAN: Don't be stupid... You're serving your country.

FIRST SS MAN: (*to* SECOND SS MAN)

    I want that blonde. I've been dreaming of breasts and hips like... (*he demonstrates*)

SECOND SS MAN: Ask her to dance with you.

FIRST SS MAN: Just like that?

SECOND SS MAN: How else can you choose?

    (*They greet the two women and begin to dance with them.*)

SECOND WOMAN: (*summoning her courage and smiling at her* SS MAN)

    So you're supposed to be a *procreator*...

SECOND SS MAN: (*laughing*) That's a fancy name... Call me Franz.

SECOND WOMAN: (*hesitating*)

    Did you choose me because there wasn't anyone else available?

SECOND SS MAN: Don't be silly... What's your name?

SECOND WOMAN: Bertha. (*They continue dancing*)

FIRST WOMAN: (*mockingly to* FIRST SS MAN)

    I'm ready, Herr Procreator.

FIRST SS MAN: Come off it. I've had my eye on you.

FIRST WOMAN: Tell me, I'll bet you're engaged to another girl.

FIRST SS MAN: (*taken aback a little*) Not really.

FIRST WOMAN: (*laughing ironically*)

    Not really? What does that mean? Still, what difference does it make? (*defiantly*) Here I am—your official, state baby-making machine.

FIRST SS MAN: (*shocked*)

> You shouldn't speak like that. You're giving your body to Germany and the Fuehrer.

SS MEN AND THE WOMEN: (*singing*)

> We are the Procreators...
> We the Baby-Making Machines...
>
> Our duty is to mate,
> For Germany create—
> Four, five, or ten...
>
> A Race of Supermen...
> And Superwomen...
>
> We are the Procreators...
> We the Baby-Making Machines...
>
> We'll make our country purer
> By mating for our Fuehrer—
> Four, five, or ten...
>
> A Race of Supermen...
> And Superwomen...

(*Eagerly they go off to their procreation tasks. The mood changes to Nazi martial music. Another banner falls reading:* THE SECRET POLICE RITUALS. *Projections of the Nazi invasions are shown.* HITLER, HIMMLER, GOERING *and* GOEBBELS *enter as if for a secret conference.*)

HITLER: France has fallen. Czechoslovakia, Hungary, Poland, Greece, Yugoslavia, belong to us. The Third Reich stretches from Norway to Africa. Are the Russian plans prepared?

GOERING: The Luftwaffe is ready, Fuehrer. The Russian air force has no possibility for serious combat. You can call me Meier if one Russian bomb ever falls on Berlin.

HITLER: (*snapping at* GOERING)

> Don't tempt me. (*He turns to* GOEBBELS.)

GOEBBELS:

> We've prepared the greatest propaganda force in the world, Fuehrer. This will be the final assault against Jewish communism.

HITLER: (*turning to* HIMMLER) What about the SS?

HIMMLER: Never before have our men been so well-trained.

HITLER: (*aside*)
> That's the only thing Himmler is good for—training secret police. (*to* HIMMLER *abruptly*) Have you prepared the Final Solution?

HIMMLER: (*uneasily*) That takes time, Fuehrer.

HITLER: (*flaring up*)
> Time? I promised the nation. If the international Jewish financiers plunge the world into another war, I promise it will be their end. The Jewish race must be annihilated.

HIMMLER:
> That is a giant task, Fuehrer. There are millions of Jews in Russia alone, three million in the Ukraine. In Poland two and a quarter million. Three quarters of a million in France. A third of a million in England. As for America...

HITLER: (*raging*) Don't tell me your numbers. I want a solution.

GOEBBELS: We must have foreign workers to man our factories.

GOERING: Draft them, send them where needed.

HITLER: Force is not enough. We need Night and Fog.

HIMMLER: Night and Fog?

HITLER: (*sharply*)
> Anyone who endangers our national security—Jew, Communist, Criminal—must be transformed into Night and Fog.

HIMMLER: (*misunderstanding*)
> We in the SS are not yet experts on the weather.

HITLER: (*snapping*)
> I'm not talking about weather. I'm talking about the function of the camps.

HIMMLER: We're doing our best. The new gas chambers at Auschwitz...

HITLER: It's not enough to kill. We need thousands of anonymous workers to produce more aircraft, tanks, artillery.

HIMMLER: We only send those prisoners unfit to work to the gas chambers. All others are segregated for forced labor.

HITLER: Work or die is not enough. You don't understand spiritual problems. We must eliminate all bourgeois ideas of personality that prevent our triumph. To achieve victory we must transform these criminal elements into Night and Fog.

> (*An* SS OFFICER *in a Deathshead uniform enters and salutes the Fuehrer. As the music of "Night and Fog" is heard, two camp prisoners, a man and a woman, almost naked, are brought in. The* SS OFFICER *examines them briefly, poking at them with his whip.*)

SS OFFICER: Your names?

MALE PRISONER: Night...(*then singing*)

> In the Night
> I lose my name.
> I am the Night...

SS OFFICER: (*to the woman prisoner*) Yours?

FEMALE PRISONER: Fog...(*then singing*)

> In the Fog
> I lose my Name.
> I am the Fog...

SS OFFICER: What do Night and Fog wear?

NIGHT: Burlap undershorts. (*As the prisoners answer the* SS OFFICER *hands them the burlap items of clothing.*)

FOG: Burlap shirt. (*They put on the shirts.*)

NIGHT: Burlap jacket. (*They put on the jackets.*)

FOG: Burlap overcoat. (*They put on the overcoats. Now they are almost identical looking—their identities vanished.*)

SS OFFICER: What are the shoes of Night and Fog?

NIGHT: Wooden clogs. (*The officer hands the prisoners the clogs.*)

SS OFFICER: What food do Night and Fog eat?

NIGHT: Warm water with cabbage leaves.

FOG: Mice if we can catch them.

SS OFFICER: How does Night catch mice?

NIGHT: I make a burlap trap. There are lots of mice in our straw beds.

SS OFFICER: Do you cook the mice?

FOG: We find some wood near the factory. We make a little fire.

NIGHT: We cook the mice in an iron saucepan.

SS OFFICER: Do you skin the mice before eating them?

NIGHT: Night eats only the meat.

SS OFFICER: You have tools for skinning?

FOG: (*quickly*) Tools are forbidden.

NIGHT:
> Night and Fog use pieces of glass, bits of iron lying around the factory.

SS OFFICER: What is the schedule of Night and Fog?

FOG: Reveille going at 4:30 AM. (*We hear the gong and roll call.*)

NIGHT: Night, here!

FOG: Fog, here!

SS OFFICER: How do Night and Fog march to work?

NIGHT:
> In ranks of five, flanked by guards and dogs, we march through the sleeping city...
>
>> (*The cadence of* Links, Recht, Links, Recht, *etc. is heard offstage as the prisoner chorus is heard singing the song:*)
>
>>> In the Night
>>> We lose our names,
>>> We lose the light,
>>> We are the Night...

SS OFFICER: No one sees you in the city?

FOG: No one sees Night and Fog.

SS OFFICER: Who knows the names, Night and Fog?

NIGHT: No one knows our names.

SS OFFICER: How long do Night and Fog work?

FOG: Twelve hours a day.

SS OFFICER: What happens to Night and Fog if they are ill?

NIGHT: They wake at dawn—in the gas chamber.

SS OFFICER: What is the religion of Night?

NIGHT: Darkness.

SS OFFICER: What is the religion of Fog?

FOG: To enter the darkness.

SS OFFICER:

> Night and Fog, Achtung! Vorwaerts Marsch! Links, Recht, Links, Recht, Links, Recht.
>
> (*He marches them out as they sing and the chorus of prisoners is heard behind them:*
>
> > In the Night
> > We lose our names
> > I am the Night,
> > I am the Fog...

CHORUS
> > In the Night
> > We lose our names,
> > We lose the light,
> > We are the Night...)

HITLER: (*to* HIMMLER)

> Night and Fog disappear into the service of the state. No information will be given out about them. Records will contain only the initials of Night and Fog. Their graves will be unmarked. You are in sole charge of the Final Solution.

HIMMLER: As you command, Fuehrer. It is a heavy task for my men.

HITLER: For strong nations history demands precedents. Only the weak permit their enemies to prosper.

HIMMLER: I understand, Fuehrer.

HITLER: Report to me when your plans are ready.

> (HIMMLER *salutes and leaves with* GOEBBBELS *and* GOERING.)

HITLER: (*brooding in the night*)

> Night and Fog surround me...Cover the stars that my destiny may triumph...Mankind has grown powerful through

HITLER CONT'D

    eternal struggle...Strength lies in attack, not defense...
    The world will only perish through eternal peace.

    (*Through the darkness* NEUMANN *steps forward. He is holding the old coat that* HITLER *wore in the opening scenes.*)

NEUMANN: (*offering* HITLER *the coat*) Here is your coat, Fuehrer.

HITLER: (*staring*) Neumann. (NEUMANN *helps him on with the coat.*)

NEUMANN: Your old Jewish peddler-friend.

HITLER: You're dead.

NEUMANN: (*smiling*)

    When you've known a Hitler it's hard to die. You can't keep me out of Night and Fog.

HITLER: (*raging*)

    You've never done anything for me, Neumann. There's no room for you in my Cathedral of Ice.

NEUMANN: (*shrugging*) I'll stand over the gate and hold your sign.

    (*He puts on the coat and hat of a Hasidic Master and moves to a top level holding the sign,* "Arbeit Macht Frei.")

HITLER: (*raging*)

    You can't hold that sign. The world will thank us for ridding the earth of you parasites.

    (*Brooding he turns his back on Neumann.*)

Scene 7—The Final Solution

(*Around the theatre a series of mysterious, contrapuntal events conflict in time, fantasies of the past that haunt the present.* HITLER *struggles to create his version of history.* NEUMANN *mocks him by playing various Hasidic Masters to show how faith survives even after the holocaust.* NIGHT AND FOG *portray their own struggle for survival. Always there is a sharp counterpoint between* HITLER'S *shaking, paranoid struggle to create his Cathedral of Ice, the forces that serve his fantasies although shaken by their own fate in time* (HIMMLER, GOERING, *the* ARCHITECT, *etc.*) *and the forces that resist his fantasies although still condemned to be part of them* (NEUMANN, NIGHT AND FOG, *etc.) All of these events flow eerily together in a fantastic collage as if the entropy of history cannot be stopped. On the upper level as* NEUMANN *transforms into a Hasidic Master, Hasidic music is heard. A disciple of the Hasidic Master is trying to dance on a ladder.*)

NEUMANN: (*mocking* HITLER *as he plays the* HASIDIC MASTER *speaking to the dancing disciple*)

    Dance, you parasite. Dance.

DISCIPLE: (*clinging desperately, afraid to dance on the ladder*)

    I'm afraid, Master. I'll fall. How can I dance on this ladder?

MASTER: Would you prefer to dance on the head of a pin? Your feet must soar from the wood.

DISCIPLE: (*puzzled, still struggling to dance*) How can I soar on a ladder?

MASTER: Man is a ladder placed on earth. Only the top of the ladder touches heaven.

DISCIPLE: (*afraid, peering up*)

    Master, I can't see the top. It's invisible. Smoke obscures the view.

MASTER: Dance through the smoke. Let joy enter your feet.

    (*Frantically the* DISCIPLE *struggles to dance.*)

MASTER: (*laughing*)

    Your feet are not even rising one inch. What good is a level dance? Dance higher. When your feet soar, when your body lifts up, your soul too will ascend.

    (*The* DISCIPLE *continues his struggle to dance higher on the ladder. After escorting the prisoners,* NIGHT AND FOG, *beneath the sign, the* SS GUARD *stops before a stand with tattooing equipment.*)

SS GUARD: (*ordering*)

    Hold out your arm. (NIGHT *draws back.*) It's only a tattoo, a little number. It doesn't hurt.

    (NIGHT AND FOG *hold out their arms and the* SS GUARD *tattoos numbers into their arms. Then the* SS GUARD *points up at the sign beside* NEUMANN.)

    See that sign. What's it say?

NEUMANN: (*reading it deliberately*) *Arbeit Macht Frei.*

NIGHT: Work makes you free.

SS GUARD: That's our motto. (*pointing*) If you can't work there's always the Perfume Factory.

(FOG *clutches her stomach*)

What's the matter?

FOG: (*hastily*) Nothing. That smell.

SS GUARD: What do you expect from a Perfume Factory? How do you feel?

FOG: (*straightening up*) I feel fine.

SS GUARD: (*to* NIGHT) How about you? You sure your health is good?

NIGHT: Yes, I want to work.

SS GUARD: Good. (*He writes on a form*) *Fit for work.* (*motioning*) You can start on the rock pile here.

(NIGHT AND FOG *start to work on the rock pile as the* SS GUARD *relaxes, watching them casually.*)

NIGHT: (*struggling with a rock*)
Why do they make roads out of such big rocks?

FOG: Don't be stupid. Maybe God wants the road to this camp made out of big rocks. (*She struggles to hoist a rock and fails.*)

NIGHT: Why call me stupid? God wouldn't be caught dead with a rock like that.

FOG: You're right. Maybe He's just here as a witness.

NIGHT: Are you crazy? Would God want to be a witness in a place like this?

(*They work in silence, eyeing the guard furtively.*)

NIGHT: (*as they work*)

If God would give you one wish now—If God would give you anything you wanted—what would you choose?

FOG: (*reflecting*) Feh, what a question. I'd choose that God would come here.

NIGHT: (*mockingly*) When should He come? Should He come tomorrow?

FOG: Tomorrow is already too late. Yesterday God should come.

> (*They continue wearily to hoist and carry rocks. Reflecting their agony* NEUMANN *begins to dance as if around a coffin, assuming the identity of the* RABBI OF BERDITCHEV.)

NEUMANN-RABBI: (*chanting*) The dance of the rocks.

FIRST DISCIPLE: (*observing, troubled*)

Look, the Rabbi of Berditchev is dancing.

SECOND DISCIPLE: It's a shame. His people are dying and he's dancing.

FIRST DISCIPLE: (*disturbed, approaches the* RABBI) Rabbi, please stop.

RABBI: (*continuing to dance*) Let me alone. Can't you see I'm dancing?

SECOND DISCIPLE: Please, Rabbi, It doesn't seem right.

FIRST DISCIPLE: Should we join you or stop you?

SECOND DISCIPLE: Which is the right way, Rabbi, that of sorrow or joy?

RABBI: (*dancing to illuminate his words*)

> The Divine Presence cannot dwell in a body of dejection. He who is truly joyful is like a man whose house has burned down. Deep in his soul he feels his need. He dances. He builds again. As he carries stones to rebuild his house, his heart rejoices. He dances with joy.
>
> (*Slowly the* DISCIPLES *join in his dance and he dances with them. Suddenly the* SS GUARD *moves toward* NIGHT AND FOG.)

SS GUARD: (*to* NIGHT)

Lawyer, you're getting too weak to work. Maybe you need another job.

NIGHT: Yes, Sir.

SS GUARD: (*calling to* SECOND SS GUARD)

Hey, Fritz, come here. (*motioning to* NIGHT) Look at his hands. He can't work anymore. He needs rest. Maybe it's time for him to become a paratrooper.

NIGHT: (*standing at attention*) What's a paratrooper, Sir?

SS GUARD: (*jovially to* SECOND SS GUARD)

He doesn't know what a paratrooper is.

SECOND SS GUARD:
    We walk you up the path there. You're on top of the rock quarry. You look around, see the beautiful view.

SS GUARD: Then you jump off into heaven.

TOGETHER: And that's how you learn to be a paratrooper.

    (*The* SS MEN *laugh.*)

SS GUARD: Listen, Jew, you're not a bad Jew. We'll give you one more chance before we turn you into a paratrooper.

NIGHT: Yes, Sir.

SS GUARD: (*pointing to* SECOND SS GUARD) You see Fritz there?

NIGHT: Yes, Sir, Herr Fritz.

SS GUARD: I'll tell you a secret about him. Fritz has a glass eye. Isn't that true, Fritz?

SECOND SS GUARD: (*smiling*) My glass eye is so perfect I can see Jews with it.

SS GUARD: (*to* NIGHT)
    If you can tell which one of Fritz's eyes is glass we'll keep you out of the paratroops.

NIGHT: (*hesitating*) That's difficult, Sir. His eyes are so clear and blue.

SS GUARD: Of course they're clear and blue. Like the sky.

NIGHT: May I move a little closer?

    (*He edges his way a little closer and studies the eyes of the* SS GUARD.)

SECOND SS GUARD: Not too close, Jew.

SS GUARD: (*impatiently*) Well, which one is glass?

NIGHT: (*pointing suddenly*) His right eye, Sir.

SECOND SS GUARD: (*angrily*) The bastard guessed right.

SS GUARD: (*to* NIGHT) You cheated. How did you find out?

NIGHT: (*tired, not caring any more*)
    You really want to know, Sir? His glass eye stands out. It looks different. It has a kindly gleam.

    (*The action freezes with the menacing sense that* NIGHT

> has gone too far. Above, NEUMANN *begins chanting and singing softly again. In his coat* HITLER *steps forward shaking to accost* HIMMLER.)

HITLER: (*to* HIMMLER) Did you ever ask yourself what is a Jew?

HIMMLER: Yes, Fuehrer, I've conducted a great deal of research in that field.

HITLER: (*looking up at* NEUMANN)

> In my Viennese years of poverty I encountered many crazy Jews like that one. I went to synagogues, listened to their whining services. I wandered down the streets where the poisonous Jewish whores of Vienna lived. I saw how they infected the city with venereal disease. How many great German geniuses died from syphilis...

NEUMANN: (*calling mockingly*) Some Jews too.

HIMMLER: Too many, Fuehrer. Nietzsche, Beethoven, Hugo Wolfe...

HITLER: (*annoyed*) I know who got syphilis.

HIMMLER: (*apologizing hastily*) I'm sorry, Fuehrer.

HITLER: I learned how Jews corrupted the newspapers, how they controlled the banks. There is only one way to stop the international Jewish conspiracy.

HIMMLER: What is that, Fuehrer?

HITLER: God must cease to exist for the Jews.

HIMMLER: (*puzzled*) We don't permit religious services for any of our Jewish prisoners.

HITLER: (*raging*) I'm not talking about praying. The Jewish God must be destroyed.

HIMMLER: (*amazed*) You think there is a Jewish God?

HITLER: (*annoyed*)

> Not to us of course. But the Jews believe in the coming of a Messiah. It gives them the strength to endure.

HIMMLER: (*suddenly beginning to understand*)

> I see. You want their faith taken away from them.

HITLER: When they lose their faith—that is the Final Solution.

(*Reacting to this* NEUMANN *becomes the* BAAL SHEM TOV. *A* DISCIPLE *approaches him.*)

FIRST DISCIPLE:
>Master, please tell me. How shall I make my living in the world?

THE BAAL SHEM: You shall be a cantor.

FIRST DISCIPLE: (*astonished*)
>A cantor? But Master, I can't even sing. I have a voice like a crow.

NEUMANN AS THE BAAL SHEM:
>With your crow's voice you'll croak with lyrical fervor. I shall bind you to the world of music. Beyond your voice shall emerge the song. They shall call you the Cantor of the Baal Shem Tov.
>
>(*Croaking at first the* DISCIPLE *begins to sing. As he continues with lyrical fervor he listens to himself with increasing joy. As the* FIRST DISCIPLE *continues singing* NEUMANN *as the* BAAL SHEM *begins to dance. After a moment the two* DISCIPLES *join in the dance. Suddenly* NEUMANN *as the* BAAL SHEM *seizes the sacred scroll of the Torah and begins to dance with it.*)

NEUMANN: Take up the Torah... Dance, sing with it...

FIRST DISCIPLE: (*shrinking back, afraid*) Look, he's dancing with the Torah!

SECOND DISCIPLE: He's gone too far. The Sacred Book is *dancing.*

(*Abruptly* NEUMANN *as the* BAAL SHEM *lays down the scroll.*)

FIRST DISCIPLE: (*whispering fearfully*) What's he doing now?

SECOND DISCIPLE: Has he lost his mind? Now he's abandoning the Torah.

(NEUMANN *as the* BAAL SHEM *begins to dance and sing again.*)

FIRST DISCIPLE:
>Look, he hasn't forgotten the Torah. Do you see what's happening to his body?

SECOND DISCIPLE: (*staring*) Grace is coming out of his flesh.

FIRST DISCIPLE: (*awed*) Fire is coming out of his body.

SECOND DISCIPLE: He has laid aside the Torah, the visible teachings.

FIRST DISCIPLE: His body is dancing with the spiritual teachings.

(*Panting, disturbed by his visionary efforts,* NEUMANN *pauses beside the sign. Below the* SECOND SS GUARD *ushers in a newly arrived prisoner, a dignified old man. Near a pile of clothes* NIGHT AND FOG *are standing with the* FIRST SS GUARD.)

SECOND SS GUARD: (*shoving the old man toward the pile of clothes*)

Go on, welcome our new arrival. Show him how my glass eye works.

FIRST SS GUARD: (*to the old man*)

He means he wants you to select your uniform. (*pointing to the pile of clothes*) You Jews like fine clothes.

SECOND SS GUARD:

Even with my glass eye I can see the quality of those clothes. You're a lucky old man to select from such a pile.

OLD MAN: (*hesitating to approach the clothes he asks* NIGHT AND FOG)

What kind of clothes are these?

NIGHT: (*whispering*) Dead men's clothes.

FOG: (*whispering, pointing furtively*)

Soon you will see the smoke. They are done for. You must wear their clothes.

OLD MAN: (*frightened*) I can't wear their clothes.

FIRST SS GUARD:

Hurry up, old man. Be careful to pick the right clothes, the best clothes for your new job.

OLD MAN: (*whispering*) What is my new job?

FOG: (*whispering*) I don't know.

SECOND SS GUARD: (*laughing*)

You'll need the best clothes you can find to cover up the smell of your new job.

(*The* GUARDS *laugh and converse together.*)

NIGHT: (*whispering to the* OLD MAN) Go on. They'll beat you.

FOG: Pick out the best clothes.

(*Slowly, fearfully, the* OLD MAN *picks out an elegant, black velvet vest and holds it up tentatively. Then as* NIGHT AND FOG *gesture encouragement to him, the* OLD MAN *begins to comprehend and pulls out a handsome, old-fashioned spring coat with silk lining.*)

FIRST SS GUARD: (*calling, laughing*) A fine spring coat, old man.

SECOND SS GUARD: (*mockingly*) He'll be a real cock of the walk.

(*The* GUARDS *laugh. Helped by* NIGHT AND FOG *the* OLD MAN *selects joyously an incredible top hat, a high hat with the rim cut off, and puts it on.*)

FIRST SS GUARD: (*breaking up with laughter*) That's a real topper.

SECOND SS GUARD: A Jewish dunce topper.

(*The* OLD MAN'S *face lights up with a radiant smile. He strikes a grand, formal pose in his ridiculous, brilliant costume.*)

FIRST SS GUARD:
Doesn't he look like a Berlin banker ready to swindle the public?

SECOND SS GUARD: Call your chauffeur, Mr. Banker.

FIRST SS GUARD: We're ready, Mr. Jew Banker. Shall we go to your bank?

SECOND SS GUARD: (*pushing the* OLD MAN *around and pointing*)
It's right there, Mr. Jew Banker. Can you smell it?

FIRST SS GUARD:
Stand in front of the latrine. You're the new *Scheissmeister*.

SECOND SS GUARD: You see that everyone shits fast on time.

FIRST SS GUARD: (*reaching into the pile of clothes and pulling out an old gold watch*)

Here's an old gold watch, Scheissmeister, to help you keep time.

SECOND SS GUARD: (*picking out a silk scarf*)
Your silk scarf to keep the stink out of your banking nose.

(*With dignity the* OLD MAN *endures the scarf being tied over his nose and mouth and the watch being put into his hand. The* GUARDS *face him toward the latrine.*)

FIRST SS GUARD: (*blowing his whistle, shouting*) Ready, Scheissmeister.

>(NEUMANN *begins to dance again, chanting softly. In an agony of stomach cramps* HIMMLER *falls before his doctor, the physical therapist,* DR. FELIX KERSTEN. *Shaking,* HITLER *watches this final series of fantasies from the side of the playing area.*)

HITLER: (*raging*) Himmler, all of this should be secret.

HIMMLER: (*clutching his stomach*)
>Dr. Kersten, please help me...I cannot breathe.

KERSTEN: Where does it hurt, Herr Himmler?

HIMMLER: (*opening his shirt, pointing to his stomach*)
>Here, here...always the same pain...(*He lies down on a couch.*)

KERSTEN: (*soothingly as he massages* HIMMLER)
>One minute. I'll help you. You know what causes these pains.

HIMMLER: These cramps are unbearable.

KERSTEN: (*kneading him like a baby*) Relax...You're tight as a drum.

HIMMLER: What would I do without you? With you I can talk in complete confidence.

KERSTEN: It is a heavy burden you carry.

HIMMLER: No one knows how heavy. The Final Solution is a purification the Fuehrer is determined to carry out.

KERSTEN: The Final Solution?

HIMMLER: No one has seen the bodies. Do you know what it is to see a pile of five hundred, a thousand bodies?

KERSTEN: I'm a doctor. I see one dead person at a time.

HIMMLER: The extermination camp is an absolute necessity. As the Fuehrer told me, we must be as strong as the Americans.

KERSTEN: (*puzzled*) The Americans?

HIMMLER: Yes, the Americans were not afraid to exterminate the Indians to secure their land. We must be as strong.

KERSTEN: (*massaging him deeply*)

But many Americans protested. Isn't there a danger? Is that better?

HIMMLER: (*with a deep sigh*)

For the first time today I can breathe without pain. No, Doctor, you forget. Only a few whites protested when Americans marched the Indians hundreds of miles to their reservations. Why should Europeans protest our difficult task with the Jews and the Russian communists?

KERSTEN: (*carefully*)

If you go on worrying like this you'll never get better. You know how badly things are going.

HIMMLER: What can I do?

KERSTEN: If you saved some of your prisoners you would be honored instead of hated. You are a powerful man. (*flattering* HIMMLER) You could earn yourself a place in history like Henry I, the German emperor you admire.

HIMMLER: Henry I. (*sitting up abruptly*) I forbid you to talk like that. It's treason. (*pointing to his SS belt buckle*) You see my SS motto—*Honor is loyalty.*

KERSTEN: (*massaging him down on the couch again to stop his protests*)

There, there. The pain will return if you agitate yourself.

HIMMLER: Do you really think I could be like Henry I?

KERSTEN: Of course, Herr Reichsfuehrer. Show the generosity of your soul.

HIMMLER: (*agitated*) Soul? Have you ever seen the soul of a Jew fly off?

KERSTEN: (*uneasily*) What do you mean?

HIMMLER: A Jew's soul is like a bat. It flaps through the sky.

KERSTEN: Really?

HIMMLER: (*rising up again in his agitation*)

The Jew's soul flaps through the sky like a giant bat. Have you ever smelled the smoke of a thousand bats burning?

KERSTEN: (*pushing him down soothingly*)

Lie down now. Your body is tense again.

HIMMLER: Kersten, your hands are the only things that help me. My stomach is burning.

KERSTEN: Rest. I'll take care of your stomach.

>(*Shaking with paranoia* HITLER *holds up his arm and the masked figure of the SS Doctor Mengele appears high up across from* NEUMANN. NEUMANN *reacts madly as* RABBI ZUSYA, *the Hasidic Master of Hanipol. He begins to scream and gesticulate with ecstasy.*)

FIRST DISCIPLE: (*anxiously to* SECOND DISCIPLE *who is reading from scripture*)

What's the matter with Rabbi Zusya?

SECOND DISCIPLE: I don't know.
>(*he tries to read from scripture*)
And God said...

>(NEUMANN-ZUSYA *pounds on the wall ecstatically and chants repetitively,* "And God said... And God said...")

FIRST DISCIPLE: (*staring*)

Zusya's lost his mind. Try to get him back to the scripture.

SECOND DISCIPLE: (*trying again*) And God said...

>(*As he continues to read the scripture it is drowned out in* ZUSYA'S *ecstatic, screaming chant of* "And God said... And God said..." *as he dances and hammers on the wall.*)

FIRST DISCIPLE: (*abruptly*) Stop reading. Don't you understand?

SECOND DISCIPLE: (*looking up, bewildered*) What?

FIRST DISCIPLE: Listen to Zusya. (*they listen*) One word is enough.

SECOND DISCIPLE: One word?

FIRST DISCIPLE: If a man speaks in the spirit of truth one word is enough.

SECOND DISCIPLE: (*as they watch* ZUSYA)

With one word the world can be redeemed.

>(*They join* ZUSYA *in his ecstatic, screaming chant and dance. Up a ramp several camp prisoners, including* NIGHT AND FOG, *the* OLD MAN, *and a* FOURTH PRISONER, *move like spectres. At the top of the ramp the SS Doctor with his riding crop motions the prisoners to the left or the right, to life or death in the gas chamber.*)

FIRST DISCIPLE: Rabbi Zusya, tell us who goes to hell, who to paradise?

ZUSYA: The bold-faced go to hell, the shame-faced to paradise.

SECOND DISCIPLE: Zusya is being God's fool again.

ZUSYA: (*praying, shouting ecstatically*)

> He who is shame-faced must beware of touching evil He must walk the heights of Paradise. He who lacks courage must cling to Heaven. But he who is bold in holiness may descend to Hell. In the alleys of shame he may live and not fear evil.
>
> (*He motions to his* DISCIPLES *to follow him. Afraid, they hesitate.*)

FIRST DISCIPLE: We are not bold-faced, Master.

SECOND DISCIPLE: How will we know which way to turn?

> (*As* NEUMANN-ZUYSA *summons them, hesitantly they follow him and join the line of camp prisoners beneath* DR. MENGELE. *In their old-fashioned Hasidic dress they make a strange contrast to the grotesque prison uniforms.*)

NIGHT: (*to* FOG, *gesturing furtively at* DR. MENGELE)

> That's Dr. Mengele. If he points to the left you die. If he points to the right you live.

FOG: How does he decide?

NIGHT: Who knows? He's a doctor. If he likes your looks.

OLD MAN: A doctor yet. He's a disgrace to his profession.

FOG: He should have had a Jewish mother.

NIGHT: What good would a Jewish mother do him?

FOG: She would have taught him not to point.

> (DR. MENGELE *signals the prisoners to approach for inspection.*)

FOURTH PRISONER: (*holding back*) I can't. I don't want to die.

OLD MAN: Don't let him see you're afraid. Death isn't the worst thing.

NIGHT: He's right. We'll meet again in a better world.

FOG: What better world?

NIGHT: (*grinning*)
>We'll meet in a shop window as soap.
>>(*As* DR. MENGELE *motions him to the left and* FOG *to the right he calls to* FOG)
>
>Don't worry about me. They'll make a sweet toilet soap from my fat.
>>(DR. MENGELE *waves the* OLD MAN *to the left and the* FOURTH PRISONER *to the right.* FOG *hesitates as if to join* NIGHT.)
>
>No, you live. Remember even soap does not forget.
>>(NIGHT *and the* OLD MAN *go off to the left,* FOG *and the* FOURTH PRISONER *to the right.* NEUMANN-ZUSYA *and his* DISCIPLES *approach beneath* DR. MENGELE'S *stare.*)

FIRST DISCIPLE: (*afraid*) Master, we are at the crossroads.

SECOND DISCIPLE: God is not here. Which way do we go?

NEUMANN-ZUSYA: (*peering up and around, shaking his head*)
>To the left is the fire. How crude is Zusya's body that it fears fire. To the right is the safety of earth. Earth, earth you are better than I. Yet I trample you with my feet. Soon I shall lie under you and be subject to you.
>>(ZUSYA *and his* DISCIPLES *begin chanting again as they await* DR. MENGELE'S *motion to the left or right. As if dream-walking* GOERING *shoulders past* HITLER *ignoring* HITLER'S *shaking protests.* GOERING *is deep in the memory of his drug addiction. Abstractly he gazes at the jewels on his fingers, at a painting he has stolen. He is dressed in an emerald-velvet, luxurious dressing gown with a giant ruby brooch pinned to the satin lapel. His face is covered with a thick layer of rouge, his fingernails lacquered a bright red. The* ARCHITECT *enters, angry and upset, trying to control himself at this late night summons from* GOERING.)

ARCHITECT: You sent for me. (*aside*) Look at him.

GOERING: (*abstractly*) Oh, it's you.

ARCHITECT: (*aside*)
>He's on heroin again. (*to* GOERING) Why did you call me here in the middle of the night?

GOERING: (*vaguely*) Yes, it came to me suddenly.

(*He extracts some diamonds and rubies from his pocket and rolls them in his hand.*)

ARCHITECT: (*impatiently*) What came to you?

GOERING: The way we can conquer.

ARCHITECT: (*incredulously, looking back at* HITLER)

Win the war? At this point? Have you told the Fuehrer about your discovery?

GOERING: Don't be so nervous. We're the technicians, eh, Architect? We'll never be defeated. Some German will always invent a new technique to save us.

ARCHITECT:

Herr Goering, I don't have much time. The situation is grave. There's a severe steel shortage.

GOERING: (*reacting*)

Don't worry. I have the solution to our problems. At heart even though he won't see me the Fuehrer knows he can trust me. (*pointing to the picture*) How do you like my new Van Dyck?

ARCHITECT: (*trying to control himself*) Very fine, but...

GOERING:

It belonged to a French Jew. He had one of the great collections. (*pointing*) Remarkable hands, don't you think?

ARCHITECT: (*impatiently*) What is your plan to win the war?

GOERING:

I haven't told the Fuehrer yet. He's a little angry with me. Is it my fault our air force suffers from lack of production? Isn't it true that enemy bombers have smashed our factories, our trains?

ARCHITECT: Yes, there's a special problem with the shortage of locomotives.

GOERING: (*lighting up with enthusiasm*)

That's what I mean. I have the solution to manufacturing locomotives. With new locomotives we'll haul supplies and build planes again. (*He lapses into vacancy.*) How do you like my jewels? If you like I'll have a brooch made for your wife.

ARCHITECT: (*trying to force him to the point*) About the locomotives.

GOERING:
> The locomotives—yes. Transportation has been the German genius. Planes, highways, buses, trains. The world has never seen such a transportation system.
>
> (*He wanders again and contemplates his jewels.*)
>
> You're wondering where my jewels came from. No, not from France. You'll never guess.

ARCHITECT: (*sharply*) What about the locomotives?

GOERING: (*dreamily*)
> Yes...Tell the Fuehrer I've solved the steel shortage. I've discovered a new material with which to build our locomotives.

ARCHITECT: What material?

GOERING: Concrete.

ARCHITECT: (*astonished*) *Concrete?*

GOERING: (*nervously rolling the jewels in his hand*)
> Concrete doesn't have the strength of steel, but we can make up for this by building more locomotives. We have no shortage of concrete.

ARCHITECT: (*sarcastically*) How would it hold together?

GOERING: (*excitedly*)
> A locomotive is crude compared with a plane. It doesn't need to hold together long. Just until we conquer.

ARCHITECT: (*carefully*) I'm afraid the weight...

GOERING: A minor problem. A concrete locomotive needn't be that heavy. You can camouflage it more easily. Don't worry, it'll work. (*another abrupt change*) Would you like to see my new painting that I acquired in the eastern campaign? I found a beautiful Vermeer, very rare you know.

ARCHITECT: (*intent on escape*)
> I'm afraid I must leave. The Fuehrer is expecting me.

GOERING: I'm glad you're going to the Fuehrer. You can tell him my plan.

ARCHITECT: (*aside*)

> The Fuehrer won't believe me if I tell him Goering has painted his fingernails red.

GOERING: Don't forget to tell the Fuehrer. (*calling louder as the* ARCHITECT *turns to flee*) Concrete locomotives, you understand, *concrete*. Use foreign slave labor to build concrete locomotives.

> (*As the* ARCHITECT *flees to the angry* HITLER, HITLER *signals again to the* SS DOCTOR *as* NEUMANN-ZUSYA *and his* DISCIPLES *face the final decision.*)

FIRST DISCIPLE: (*fearfully*) Rabbi Zusya, which is the path to heaven?

NEUMANN-ZUSYA: (*trembling*) The way to the fire is the path to heaven.

SECOND DISCIPLE: (*pointing to* MENGELE) Is that the Devil?

NEUMANN-ZUSYA: Inside the uniform is a man.

FIRST DISCIPLE: I can see only the uniform.

NEUMANN-ZUSYA:
> I will show you the man. (*He approaches the* SS DOCTOR) Sir, you have light coming out of you.

SS DOCTOR: Back!

NEUMANN-ZUSYA: (*kneeling and stretching out his hand*)   Let me touch you.

SS DOCTOR: (*striking* NEUMANN *down with his whip*)

> How dare you touch me, Jew.

NEUMANN-ZUSYA: (*rebounding radiantly*)

> Sir, I envy you. When you turn to God each of your flames will become a ray of holy light. (*screaming*) *And God said: A great light will shine*...

DISCIPLES: (*they begin to scream with* NEUMANN-ZUSYA)

> And God said: A great light will shine...

NEUMANN-ZUSYA: (*through the* DISCIPLES' *voices*)

> Sir, I envy you your flood of holy radiance...*And God said*... *And God said*...

> (*The* DISCIPLES *join him in the words,* "*And God said.*" *As the* SS DOCTOR *motions angrily they continue with*

> ZUSYA *to repeat these words. The* SS GUARDS *lead* NEUMANN-ZUSYA *and his* DISCIPLES *off left to the gas chamber.*)
>
> (HITLER *moves, shaking, toward* EVA BRAUN. *It is as if they are in their final nightmare in the Berlin Bunker.*)

HITLER: That's the end of Neumann. I'll show him how to die. (*bitterly to* EVA) The German people have betrayed me. I trained them to be strong. I trained them to be merciless. They've become weak. We must show the world how we died, how we live on.

EVA: What are you going to do?

HITLER: I'm going to marry you.

EVA: Another wedding. Oh, thank you, Adolf.

HITLER: And then we're going to kill ourselves.

EVA: (*entranced*) *Liebestod*...

HITLER: Greater than *Liebestod*...Wagner is only a composer. I'm an architect of new societies. (*motioning*) Take down my will. (*hastily she gets a notebook*) Of my own free will I choose immortality.

EVA: (*looking up*) What about me?

HITLER: (*impatiently motioning to her to continue*)

> In the Cathedral of Ice I have decided to take as my wife the woman who, after many years of faithful friendship...

EVA: (*looking up*) Of love, of love...

HITLER: (*ignoring this*)

> ...of faithful friendship, entered this place in order to share my fate. Our death will compensate us for the companionship we have lost through my work in the service of my people who have proved themselves unfit to achieve victory.
>
> (*She nods assent and he launches into a more vehement attack*)
>
> In the future I charge the world leaders to scrupulous ob-

HITLER CONT'D

    servance of the laws of race. I demand their merciless opposition to the universal poisoner of all peoples—International Jewry. From our death will spring the renaissance of our National Socialist movement. We shall not fail to realize a true community of nations. Our spirit will endure forever...

EVA: (*beginning to understand*) We will become immortal...

HITLER: Wherever men dream they will think of me. My Nazi Fantasies will triumph.

EVA: (*writing exultantly*) The Nazi Fantasies will triumph.

HITLER: Wherever men speak of politics, power, art, they will speak of me. (*He shows her a poison capsule and a pistol.*)

EVA: What are those?

HITLER: Here is your poison... The pistol is mine.

EVA: (*shrinking back a little*)

    You promised to marry me. Don't forget to marrry me first...

HITLER: (*exultantly*)

    Marriage, why not? Love—Death...Immortality...My Nazi Fantasies triumph in the Cathedral of Ice...

    (*He tears his coat off, throws it away, then signals and the Dream Machine erupts—with all of The Power Fantasies occurring simultaneously in the niches.*)

    (*In the first niche* KARL MAY *dressed as* OLD SHATTERHAND *repeats and elaborates on his cry:* "I am great...I am mar—vel—ous!...")

    (*In the second niche the* ARCHITECT, *slowly, maniacially as if condemned in time, hammers at a model of one of* HITLER'S *monuments, crushing it into perfect ruins.*)

    (*In the third niche a dream version of Mephistopheles drops a variety of incredible paper superbombs on* GOERING-MEIER *who is forced to keep dodging as if pestered by eternal mosquitos.*)

    (*In the fourth niche* SCHRECK, *the chauffeur, drives madly through time.*)

    (*In the fifth niche* WAGNER *conducts grandly.*)

(*In the sixth niche* NAPOLEON *presides over a dance of power with* STALIN, ROOSEVELT *and* CHURCHILL.)

(*In the seventh niche the* KING OF THE MOUNTAIN *hunches over his tape recorder trying to penetrate the dream-sounds of the taped voices that echo forever in his mind.*)

(*In the eighth niche* NEUMANN *as one of the* HASIDIC MASTERS *looks down on* KERSTEN *massaging the pain-wracked stomach of* HIMMLER.)

(*In the ninth niche* GOEBBELS *and his wife stare at each other over the poisoned bodies of their children like a Geman Macbeth and Lady Macbeth.*)

(*In the tenth niche* CHARLEMAGNE *appears in an imperial dream-pose.*)

(*At the climax of the simultaneous Fantasies of Power the entire cast sings "The Ballad of the Cathedral of Ice"*)

HITLER AND CAST: Charlemagne!
Rise from your tomb.
Dreams have no price.
Power lives on
In my Cathedral of Ice.

CAST: Charlemagne!
Come buy your joy or sorrow.
In the Cathedral of Ice
We freeze you for tomorrow...

(*The actors freeze in their niches in dream-like attitudes of power as the actor who plays* HITLER *steps forward. He takes off his mustache, brushes back his hair, and resumes his role as* NARRATOR *to say farewell to the audience.*)

NARRATOR: Good night, ladies and gentlemen...
Sweet dreams with your dreams of power...
The clocks begin to send us into space;
Our dreams still soar to rule each waking face...
Who we are, what we hope to be
We learn behind the masks of history—
We wish you well—and praise the stage
Where we meet to celebrate our joy, our rage...

(*After the initial applause the entire cast sings the final stanzas of "The Ballad of the Cathedral of Ice"*)

NARRATOR AND CAST:

    Charlemagne!
    Into history, into time,
    Our troops march on
    Forever into dream.

    Charlemagne!
    Come buy your joy or sorrow.
    In the Cathedral of Ice
    We freeze you for tomorrow...

THE END

Of this first edition of 650 copies
150 are hardbound, numbered
and signed by the author.

James Schevill